Learning Outdoors

Also available:

Playing Outside
Activities, Ideas and Inspiration for the Early Years
Helen Bilton
ISBN 1 84312 067 4

Outdoor Play in the Early Years (Second Edition)
Management and Innovation
Helen Bilton
ISBN 1 85346 952 1

Organising Play in the Early Years
Practical Ideas for Practitioners
Jane Drake
ISBN 1 84312 025 9

Planning Children's Play & Learning in the Foundation Stage (Second Edition)
Jane Drake
ISBN 1 84312 151 4

The Early Years Curriculum
A View from Outdoors
Gloria Callaway
ISBN 1 84312 345 2

Learning Outdoors

Improving the quality of young children's play outdoors

Edited by Helen Bilton

Contributions from Karen James, Jackie Marsh, Anne Wilson and Maggie Woonton

Routledge
Taylor & Francis Group

LONDON AND NEW YORK

First published 2005 by David Fulton Publishers

This edition reprinted 2010 by Routledge
2 Park Square, Milton Park, Abingdon, Oxon, OX14 4RN
711 Third Avenue, New York, NY 10017

Routledge is an imprint of the Taylor & Francis Group, an informa business

Note: The right of the individual contributors to be identified as the authors of their work has been asserted
by them in accordance with the Copyright, Designs and Patents Act 1988.

Copyright © Helen Bilton, Karen James, Jackie Marsh, Anne Wilson and Maggie Woonton 2005

British Library Cataloguing in Publication Data
A catalogue record for this book is available from the British Library

ISBN: 978-1-843-12350-7 (pbk)

Contents

Foreword   vii

Acknowledgements   ix

About the authors   xi

Preface   xiii

Introduction   xv

Background to the Brent Outdoor Play Project   xvii

Section 1   Outdoor Learning in Practice   **1**

1   Deciding on the size and scope of your project   1

2   Planning and resourcing outdoor play   11

3   Creating the outdoor learning environment   25

4   What do children learn outdoors?   45

5   Barriers and solutions   67

6   Benefits of outdoor play   75

Section 2   Forms and Checklists   **79**

Section 3   Further Ideas and Materials to Develop Outdoor Provision **85**

Bibliography   101

Useful contacts   103

Index   105

Foreword

In common with many parts of the country, in Brent we celebrate the diversity and cultural richness of the population. As with the whole of London, ours is a very young population, with a projected increase in the population of children aged under 5, which is out of step with the trend in England as a whole. Early education and childcare provision in Brent has grown steadily in line with a strong local commitment to nursery education and with the National Childcare Strategy.

We embarked on the Outdoor Play Project because we believed that there was more to be achieved in outdoor provision in Brent; we hoped to draw on the creativity and experience of practitioners, and to look outdoors with a fresh perspective.

Our project included settings of all types. The project group was self-selecting, with all practitioners aiming to improve the experiences of their children. It emerged, however, that the experiences of adults were also affected. In some settings, the project simply dispelled the tacitly held belief that learning acquired indoors is somehow superior to learning acquired outdoors. In some settings, the project addressed the quality of the environment as a whole, in some the assessment of learning, and in others it became the catalyst for key-stage and whole-school review.

The very diversity that we celebrate here brings with it a multitude of approaches, experiences and beliefs about nursery education and childcare, among both practitioners and parents. Our role was to challenge practitioners to make the changes they needed to in order to make these environments a reality, and to empower them to have the debate that would sustain them in doing so. One of the positive outcomes of the debate we raised in Brent was the opening of our first children's centre, where children can spend the entire session outdoors, choosing when to go inside.

Lesley Fox-Lee
Head of Early Years
London Borough of Brent

Acknowledgements

We would like to thank: Marjorie Ouvry for sowing the seeds of enthusiasm for outdoor play in Brent; Kathryn Solly, Chelsea Open Air Nursery, for her wealth of ideas and expertise; and Lucky Khera, Strathmore Infants, Hertfordshire, for generously sharing her ideas and experiences.

The book celebrates the achievements of all the project settings – all the practitioners, parents and the children who embraced outdoor play so enthusiastically and without whom this book would not exist. The settings and project leaders that took part in the project are listed below:

Anansi Nursery – Daksha Patel
Abbey Nursery – Ruby Azam
Barnhill Nursery – Liz Watkins and Sandra Warwick
Bluebell Nursery – Alka Desai
Carlton Centre Nursery – Cecilia Mensah
Christchurch C. of E. Primary School – Cheryl Green
College of North West London Nursery – Maida Najafi and Joanne Davies
College Green Nursery – Althea Owens-Maxwell
Convent of Jesus & Mary Infant School – Anne McBrearty and Martina Daniels
Curzon Crescent Nursery – Bernie Clark
Donnington Primary School – Jackie Smith
Evan Davies Nursery – Linda Mitchell and Bernard Gumley
Fryent Primary School – Michelle Workman and Wendy Fuller
Gower House School – Joy Andrews
Happy Days Montessori Nursery – Trusha Shah and Margaret Dillane
Hopscotch Nursery – Fung Ng
Jellitots Nursery – Sarah Crawford and Wendy Kelly
Kingsbury Jewish Kindergarten – Rebecca Moses
Learning Tree Montessori Nursery – Roshina Karmay
Little Acorn Nursery – Beverley Demetrius
Mount Stewart Primary School – Geraldine Murphy
North West London Jewish Day School – Frances Smith
Roe Green Infants – Marina Aziz
St Mary's Nursery – Alice Alves and Kathryn Butler-Lloyd
Torah Temimah – Hannah Lopez
University of Westminster Nursery – Surita Gupta

We were also given additional material by:

Harlesden Primary School
Heather Park Nursery
Kenton Kindergarten
Little Angels Nursery

About the authors

Maggie Woonton, Anne Wilson, Jackie Marsh and Karen James are all Early Years Advisory Teachers in Brent.

Maggie is both a teacher and a nursery nurse and has worked in the UK and abroad, within health, social services and community provision.

Anne has a wealth of early years experience and is keen to promote high quality provision by developing a rich learning environment.

Jackie has worked in a variety of early years settings and trained early years practitioners. She is particularly interested in children under three.

Karen has worked in the Foundation Stage for many years. The impact of practitioner research on practice is her particular interest.

The Editor, Helen Bilton, is an educational consultant, adviser and trainer.

Preface

The Outdoor Play Project has come about through the sheer determination of Lesley Fox-Lee, Head of Early Years in Brent. She has been the driving force behind the project and this publication.

Anne, Jackie, Karen and Maggie, the Brent Early Years Advisory Teachers, have made this project actually happen and have put in all the hard work, supporting practitioners in their endeavours. They have also written this book – a superb achievement! They have been a delight to work with – always obliging, caring, happy and helpful, with children at the centre of their thoughts and ideas. They have been quietly inspirational.

The staff involved in the project have been enthusiastic, thoughtful and courageous – always willing to give it a go. I take my hat off to them all!

I hope this handbook will be useful as a blueprint for setting up an Outdoor Play Project anywhere, whether it be on a borough-wide basis or in your own early years setting.

Helen Bilton
July 2005

Introduction

We have written this handbook with practitioners and Early Years Advisory Teachers in mind. During this project we came into contact with many organisations and practitioners and we have acquired a range of materials and ideas that we would like to share with you.

Although we worked mainly with two- to five-year-olds, we feel that the principles apply also to babies and older children. We considered issues of equality and, in the spirit of inclusion, have threaded them throughout the text. Wherever reference is made to parents we include all carers and family members who look after children.

The book is organised into three sections:

Section 1 contains information about the project – its background, development and impact – and is divided into six chapters.

- **Chapter 1** examines the different ways you can approach the development of your outdoor area from small-scale quick changes to long-term development plans.
- **Chapter 2** examines the different ways to approach the planning and resourcing of outdoor areas.
- **Chapter 3** shows how the outdoor area can be organised and managed. It describes the way the environment can be set out as provision bays and suggests basic equipment and learning possibilities.
- **Chapter 4** examines the children's learning that takes place in the outdoor areas, particularly the learning which can only take place outdoors, and ways to extend the learning taking place indoors.
- **Chapter 5** considers the difficulties and barriers and offers solutions to common problems.
- **Chapter 6** highlights the benefits of outdoor play. It considers the significant implications for the children, practitioners and parents.

Section 2 contains pro formas and focus sheets that can be used in training or staff meetings. Adaptable versions of these pro formas can be downloaded from the publisher's website: http://www.routledgeteachers.com

Section 3 contains practical ideas and suggestions.

We hope that you enjoy your journey through the book and that you and the children spend many hours learning together with the 'sky as your roof' (McMillan 1930: 16).

Background to the Brent Outdoor Play Project

This chapter sets out the background to Brent's Outdoor Play Project, from its beginning at the Early Years Annual Conference in March 2003 to the celebration of achievement in July 2004. The decision to focus on learning outdoors at the annual conference, and the project that arose from this, were influenced by several factors, both national and local. These included the statutory requirements, key issues from Ofsted reports, and research findings about children's sedentary lifestyles and lack of physical exercise. There was also a general concern about children's well-being because of the length of time spent in a setting with little or no access to the outdoors. 'Children are losing their connection with the natural environment and their well being and environmental quality are inextricably linked' (Thomas and Thompson 2004). The Play Charter (Children Now 2004), supported by a number of associations, states, 'it is essential that children have easy access to outdoor space for spontaneous physical activity.'

This chapter briefly explores issues concerning:

- Outdoor play as a statutory requirement
- Relevant research
- Consequences for learning, gender and additional needs
- The local picture in Brent.

Outdoor play as a statutory requirement

The *Curriculum Guidance for the Foundation Stage* (QCA 2000) emphasises that the outdoors is as much a part of a child's learning environment as the indoor environment. This document states that every child should have access to an outdoor curriculum. The principles state: 'To be effective, an early years curriculum should be carefully structured. Planned and purposeful activity ... provides opportunities for teaching and learning, both indoors and **outdoors**' (QCA 2000: 11).

In expounding these principles, the document proposes that a planned and carefully structured curriculum should provide rich and stimulating experiences and 'make good use of **outdoor space** so that children are enabled to learn by working on a larger, more active scale than is possible indoors' (QCA 2000: 15). In addition, the document makes the statement: 'Well-planned play, both indoors and **outdoors**, is a key way in which young children learn with enjoyment and challenge' (QCA 2000: 25).

References to the importance of the outdoor area for young children are made throughout the document in each of the six areas of learning. For example:

- **Personal, social and emotional.** 'An environment indoors and **outdoors** where children feel secure, valued, confident and independent' (QCA 2000: 31).
- **Communication, language and literacy.** 'Giving opportunities for linking language with physical movement in ... practical experiences such as ... gardening' (QCA 2000: 44).
- **Mathematics.** 'It is important to provide a rich environment **outdoors** as well as indoors, in which children are provided with interesting materials to sort, count, talk about, compare, use for making models and so on' (QCA 2000: 72).

- **Knowledge and understanding of the world.** Provide 'an environment with a wide range of activities indoors and **outdoors** that stimulate children's interests and curiosity' (QCA 2000: 82). 'Making effective use of the **outdoors** and the local neighbourhood' (QCA 2000: 84).
- **Physical development.** Provide 'opportunities for regular and frequent physical activity indoors and **outdoors**' (QCA 2000: 102).
- **Creative development.** References to children playing outdoors are made in the section 'Examples of what children do', such as children collecting leaves and sticks to make a 'big nest' (QCA 2000: 126).

The House of Commons Select Committee (January 2001) report on the early years also highlighted the importance of learning outdoors. Its recommendations were that 'to meet the requirements of the Early Learning Goals, every setting that is inspected by Ofsted should have sufficient space outdoors available to the children' (Ofsted 2001: 24).

Ofsted reports, both nationally and locally, have indicated that this was an area that could be developed in many settings, and noted that some did not have dedicated areas for outdoor play.

Research findings concerned with lifestyles

Playing out

Concerns have been raised nationally about children's sedentary lifestyles. Marjorie Ouvry (speaking at the Brent Early Years Annual Conference 2003) suggested that many children live in cramped home conditions that can restrict their movement, and that many of the traditional places where children used to play freely are now lost to them. She concluded that some parents are reluctant to let their children use local parks, which they consider unsafe, or to play in the street in front of their houses for fear of abduction or of traffic. Today, children are often driven to school or nursery, and so they lose the opportunities that walking once afforded for physical exercise as well as the social interaction with their friends – both important sources of learning.

Alternatives to 'playing out' are computer games and television viewing, which are much more part of our culture than they once were. Many children spend long hours in the home engaged in solitary play or in sedentary occupations. Goddard-Blythe (2000) suggests that hours spent in front of the television provide children with a 'surfeit of stimulation', but no physical interaction. She argues:

> These children run the risk of later specific learning difficulties, behavioural and social problems not because they lack intelligence, but because the basic systems fundamental to academic learning are not fully in place when they begin school. Attention, Balance and Co-ordination are the primary ABC on which all later learning depends. (Goddard-Blythe 2000: 23)

Food

This lack of exercise, plus the greater consumption of junk food and foods with a high fat content, has led to an increase in instances of obesity. The Department of Health research (2004) shows that incidences of obesity in under 4s have grown to 9 per cent in 1998 for two- to four-year-olds. This has nearly doubled in the ten years since 1989. Linked with this is a similar rise in cases of diabetes in this age group. Around 50 per cent of children do not engage in one hour a day of physical activity. 'Lack of regular, vigorous exercise is resulting in children as young as three showing signs of heart disease' (Tovey 1999: iii).

As a result of these concerns, we decided to investigate research into how children learn through movement, particularly using the outdoor environment. The research further strengthened our resolution to promote outdoor play as being essential to young children's development.

Consequences for learning

Movement

The lack of opportunities for children to play outdoors and the consequent lack of movement has implications not only for their physical development but also for their learning in the social, emotional and cognitive domains. The Curriculum Guidance for the Foundation Stage states: 'At first, all learning arises from physical action and the gathering of experience through the senses' (QCA 2000: 45). Gallahue and Ozmun write:

> Children's play is the primary mode by which they learn about their bodies and movement capabilities. It also serves as an important facilitator of cognitive and affective growth in the young child. Children learn most effectively about themselves, other people and the world when they are actively using all their senses and movement within a supportive environment. (Gallahue and Ozmun 1998: 193)

This endorses Brearley's (1969) research that children's emotional, intellectual and physical growth is linked to movement and that what they feel, think and do can all be looked at in movement terms. Ouvry (speaking at the Early Years Conference 2003) highlighted the point that if children are to gain full control over their muscles and involuntary movements they have to be active and that outdoor play exercises both 'muscles and minds'. Bruce points out that practitioners should provide children with plenty of rich experiences within a supportive environment so they can 'make sense of the way they use their senses and movement' (Bruce 2004a: 127).

Learning through movement is essential from birth onwards. Davies (2003:13) argues that 'freedom of movement means freedom to learn'. As babies move their heads, bodies and limbs, their brains receive kinaesthetic feedback. This enables babies to begin to make meaning of their experiences and to learn from them. The sights, smells and patterns outdoors are key ways that babies can develop their sense-making capacities. Goswami's (2004) research linking movement and babies' and young children's brain development reinforces the appropriateness of outdoor play, where learning through kinaesthetic paths is particularly effective.

The idea of learning through movement is not new. In the 1920s the nursery pioneers had seen movement as the main way by which young children learn. Margaret McMillan recognised that 'children want space at all ages ... to move, to run, to find things out by new movement, to feel one's life in every limb, that is the life of early childhood' (McMillan 1930 in Ouvry 2001: 14). This vision inspired our ambition to promote outdoor play in current early years provision. Susan Isaacs reiterated this, saying:

> Little children need space, both for their physical efforts and so that they shall not be too much in each other's way and annoy each other by contact or noise. To be boxed up in the small nursery ... is a very trying experience for vigorous,

healthy children of three to five years of age and a source of great irritation and nervous strain. Space has in itself a calming and beneficent effect. (Isaacs 1954: 29)

This still applies for our children today.

Gender

Other research reveals that some boys, who are at risk of becoming disaffected at a very young age, have shown significant improvements if their learning takes place outdoors. Given the choice, boys often choose to spend more time in activities involving high levels of physical activity. Henniger (1985) found that the dramatic play of boys was strongly influenced by the outdoor environment and that they engaged in more of this type of play outdoors. His research showed that some children were inhibited by being indoors. This was because the limitations of space and allowable noise prevented the more active types of play that encouraged some boys to engage in higher levels of social play such as co-operative play.

Much recent research has focused on how the brain works. This has shown that boys' brains mature in a different sequence to girls' and, in some areas, at a slower rate. This can have a direct bearing on how boys learn. Boys first develop the part of the brain for knowing about movement and the space in which they move themselves and other things. Consequently, they generally feel more secure in the outdoor environment where there is space for them to learn through movement and where they are more likely to engage in the more formal aspects of the curriculum.

Although the outdoor environment may be central in helping boys, it appears that in terms of equality of opportunities this is not happening for girls. Cullen (1993) found that the play of boys and girls outdoors followed the stereotype established indoors, with boys playing with the more active equipment and girls tending to stay with the more home-type play. During the outdoor play project, Helen Bilton discussed the role of the adult in her second session with the project leaders. She suggested that the role of the adult was to model and promote non-stereotypical play, and she saw this as critical in including girls in more active play. Browne (2004) urges us to consider results of gender research with caution and to be aware that neither boys nor girls are homogeneous groups.

Children with disabilities or additional needs were often overprotected and not given access to outdoor play on a regular basis. In Brent we felt that such children would benefit greatly from having regular access to the outdoors and deemed it important to include them in the project. As Lady Allen of Hurtwood suggested, play opportunities have not sufficiently considered the needs of disabled children. 'Physically handicapped children often lead an unnecessarily limited life. They are often over protected and are rarely allowed to take risks' (John and Wheway 2004: 6).

The local picture in Brent

Brent mirrors many of the national issues, and all these concerns contributed to our decision to focus on learning outdoors. This section of the chapter explains the background to our project and should be of particular interest to LEAs that are considering setting up their own outdoor play project.

In September 2003, the Early Years Service in Brent embarked on a project to raise the profile of outdoor play in its Foundation Stage settings. Practitioners from the maintained and non-maintained sectors were invited to the first session in the Autumn term and subsequently committed to a year-long development programme, during which they would examine their outdoor play and record their progress.

The initial conference

Interest in learning outdoors had arisen from a very successful conference. Participants were drawn from the maintained, private, independent and voluntary sectors. Some registered childminders also attended. Marjorie Ouvry provided the keynote speech at the conference, emphasising that the outdoor environment provides opportunities for learning in all the areas of the curriculum and that access to the outdoors in all weathers was an entitlement for each child.

The message that delegates received from the workshops they attended endorsed these points: the outdoors could offer children space to move freely and to use the whole of their bodies to find out about the world and to test out their growing capabilities in a secure but challenging and enabling environment. The full potential of learning outdoors was made very clear, including the fact that some learning can only happen outside.

Evaluations of the conference and subsequent visits to settings by the Early Years Advisory Team showed that for many the conference was an inspiration to them and they had started to develop their outdoor areas, implementing what they had seen and heard.

Setting up the project

Building on this interest and further requests for support, the Early Years Service set up the outdoor play project to develop learning outdoors. The project aimed to support and develop practice in a variety of settings and to document practitioners' progress over the period of a year. Helen Bilton was invited to lead the development of the project. Three sessions, one per term, were planned with Helen. Drawing on her experience of outdoor play and of supporting other LEAs in setting up similar projects, Helen inspired, motivated and encouraged the project leaders to develop their outdoor play areas.

The central training programme offered further support for practitioners, with workshops on the organisation and management of the outdoor area from Kathryn Solly, Head of Chelsea Open Air Nursery School.

Who took part in the project?

Twenty-six settings opted to take part. These included the following:

- Fifteen private nurseries
- Nine schools in the maintained sector and two from the independent sector. One of the schools had a fee-paying playgroup within its early years unit and the playgroup, nursery and reception classes were able to work together to develop their outdoor space.

Twenty-five of the settings had outdoor spaces or the possibility of acquiring space. Some had specially designed outdoor areas; others had an area where they could set up equipment on a permanent basis; others had to store equipment away each day. Only one setting had no access to an outdoor space.

Spaces were used in different ways. For some settings the outdoor area was used for a limited time each day; for others longer sessions were available if the weather was fine. Some settings only took their children out in the summer months.

Qualifications and training of staff were diverse and included Montessori-trained teachers, practitioners with NVQ Levels 2 and 3 and qualified teachers.

Some managers and head teachers made it possible for two practitioners to attend the course. This gave the practitioners a greater sense of being valued and supported, not only by each other but also by their setting.

Participants were asked to keep a record of their progress and were issued with digital cameras to encourage them to record what was happening. Settings charted their own progress through photographs, diaries, observations and comments made by staff, parents and children.

Part of the last training day was a sharing of progress and a discussion of significant development. The enthusiasm and excitement shown by practitioners were palpable as they reflected on their practice. This enabled them to realise what they had achieved over the year and to recognise the positive effects it had had on them, the children and other members of staff.

OUTDOOR LEARNING IN PRACTICE

1 Deciding on the size and scope of your project

In this chapter we will be looking at the various ways of approaching the development of outdoor provision. Some settings may want to redesign a whole area involving a long-term plan, others may want to develop a specific aspect or need a 'quick change' approach such as collecting many recycled materials and organising them in bays. Whether you have a designated outdoor area leading off from the main nursery room or a tarmac space between the front gate and the door, there's always plenty of options for change and improvement.

The following examples and ideas illustrate the diverse approaches taken by some of the settings in the Brent outdoor play project. They are presented in a variety of styles, which reflect the different ways the projects developed.

A complete overhaul in a year

Context

This privately run full-day nursery caters for 30 children between the ages of 2 and 5 and is held in a church hall. The practitioners have to clear away at the end of each day and they do not have a designated outdoor area. At the beginning of the project, they were using a small, grassed area at one side of the hall and part of the car park. They recognised the need to develop their outdoor provision and so booked a place on the outdoor play project. The following account is taken from the diary kept by the team during the year of the project.

The starting point

The outdoor space consists of a large tarmac area of driveway, which practitioners cordon off with a portable wooden fence (Figures 1.1 and 1.2). In the past they took the toys and equipment outside during the morning and invited the children to 'come and play' for short periods of time.

Figure 1.1 A space to run and play

Figure 1.2 The outside area before it was developed

After attending the first day of training, practitioners got together and began to think in more detail about the changes that could be planned. They came up with the following overall aim (Figure 1.3) and then began to decide on the improvements they would like to make and how to go about making these changes happen.

Overall aim:
To make the outdoor area a more interesting and stimulating place for children to be, and for staff and children to see it as an extension of the nursery, encouraging everyone to spend more time outside.

Improvements we would like to make:
1. Create a quiet area where children can sit and talk to each other or read books.
2. Introduce a sensory area with mirrors, wind chimes, musical instruments, a weaving frame and a planting area.
3. Turn the shady space into a nature area, using logs and bark, and grow wildlife-friendly plants so that children can observe mini-beasts in their natural habitat.

Figure 1.3 Our overall aim

What happened

1. One member of the team attended the Outdoor play project.

2. On her return to the setting, a meeting was organised to discuss outdoor provision.

3. During the meeting, practitioners drew up an action plan.

4. In order to raise the money needed to fund the developments they organised fund raising events, including a raffle and a Christmas concert.

5. New pieces of large equipment were sourced and bought, including an outdoor storage cupboard and storage boxes.

6. They gave the environment a 'face lift' by painting the fence and playhouse. They also painted numbers on the fence.

7. Practitioners were finding it exhausting getting resources together and taking them out each day, so they thought about different ways they could manage this. The advisory teacher suggested creating boxes of resources for each of the bays. This would allow the children a wide range of materials with which to work, which could be packed away each day, stored overnight and got out again the following day.

8. At another staff meeting they decided who would be responsible for each of the bays.

9. They decided on a budget for the bays and shared thoughts on what to put in each.

We placed chipped bark on the ground in this small shady corner to create a nature area. The addition of a large tree stump, several logs, a bird table, a bee house and a ladybird hotel ensured a habitat for many mini-beasts. Laminated photographs of garden creatures and poems about insects were put around the area. Lavender and Bergamot bushes were planted to attract bees and butterflies. Initially we had a few problems with plants being trampled on and logs being

Figure 1.5 Reading poems in our nature area

removed from the area. By working in the area with the children, we showed them how to look at plants, bugs and insects and encouraged them to examine, describe, draw and identify what they had found. The children responded well to this and have been showing a real interest in the caterpillars, slugs, snails and ladybirds they have found. They are learning how to handle them carefully and think about the physical needs of all creatures.

Figure 1.4 Creating a nature area

10. They set about collecting materials for the boxes for each bay.

11. As they got the materials together they set up the bays.

12. Construction workers on a neighbouring building site provided the setting with logs and gravel, which formed the basis of their natural area.

13. One of the most successful additions to the garden (and also the cheapest) has been the provision of large equipment such as planks, tyres, crates and boxes, which have been combined with resources such as ropes, dressing-up clothes and fabric. These additions have formed the basis for many imaginative games (Figure 1.6). They began by arranging the planks, tyres, etc. but gradually the children have taken the initiative and created their own constructions.

We have been amazed at the children's creativity and resourcefulness. Their imaginative play has become much richer now that they have more resources and space to play in.

These resources have also provided opportunities for the children to develop aspects of their physical development, such as balancing, lifting and carrying. The children are thinking more about safety and working together co-operatively.

A long-term plan

Context

This setting was a large inner-city faith-based primary school with a nursery unit on site. The Nursery unit is separate from the Reception class.

Figure 1.6 A Power Ranger house

What happened

The Foundation Stage Co-ordinator, who is also the Reception teacher, attended the training. She left enthused and was determined to make changes to the space used by the children in the Reception class.

1. After discussion with the staff team, visits were organised to other early years settings in order to glean ideas and gain information about the many different possibilities available.

2. Following the visits, meetings were organised with the head teacher and the chair of governors, to share the information with them. A commitment was made by the school to develop the outdoor area. This commitment was supported by money being allocated to the project from the School Improvement Plan Budget.

3. This resulted in a long-term project being developed.

4. The practitioners were particularly interested in having a canopy that would enable the children to use the area at all times of the year. With this in mind, they planned visits to particular early years settings to look at 'canopies in situ', and the chair of the governing body agreed that the canopy was an essential aspect of the development plan.

5. In the light of their visits, the staff team devised a 'wish list' of features they would like to include in the area. They particularly liked the idea of sliding doors, which enable children to move in and out even when the weather is cold. Another impressive feature was the development of raised and sunken areas, which would add interest for the children within the confines of their relatively small space.

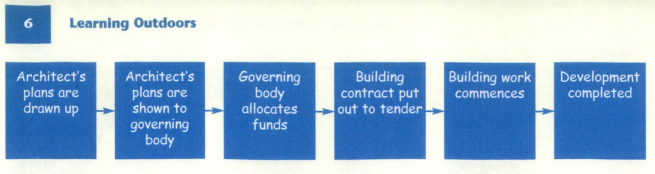

Figure 1.7 Development timeline

6. 'Creating a stimulating outdoor environment for the Reception children' became an agenda item at a governors' meeting, and this resulted in an architect's involvement.

7. An architect was commissioned to draw up plans.

8. Meetings between the staff, the head teacher and members of the governing body were organised to decide on the budget and a timeline was devised (Figure 1.7).

Responding to an Ofsted inspection

Context

In this three-form entry infant school, only one of the Reception classes had direct access to the outdoor provision. This was mainly tarmac and was used by all the infant classes at break times and lunch times. Although the Reception classes used this space throughout the day, the constraints of only one adult per class meant that access had to be timetabled. This made it impossible to allow children free flow play indoors or outdoors.

What happened

In response to an Ofsted inspection, the Foundation Stage team explored ways in which the children in the Reception classes could learn outdoors. A plan to share the outdoor area of the Nursery was developed and implemented (Figure 1.8).

Quick-change approach

Context

This is a privately owned neighbourhood nursery catering for 85 children from 6 months to 5 years of age. In this setting, the manager attended the training. This had an immediate impact on the progress of the project, as she developed an action plan and began work on it straight away.

Recipe for change

1. Attend training – take lots of notes and prepare yourself to disseminate the information gained.

2. Organise a staff meeting shortly after the training.
    ■ Share with the staff team the information gained.
    ■ Generate enthusiasm for change.
    ■ Identify team of 'change agents'.
    ■ Set targets and date for next meeting.

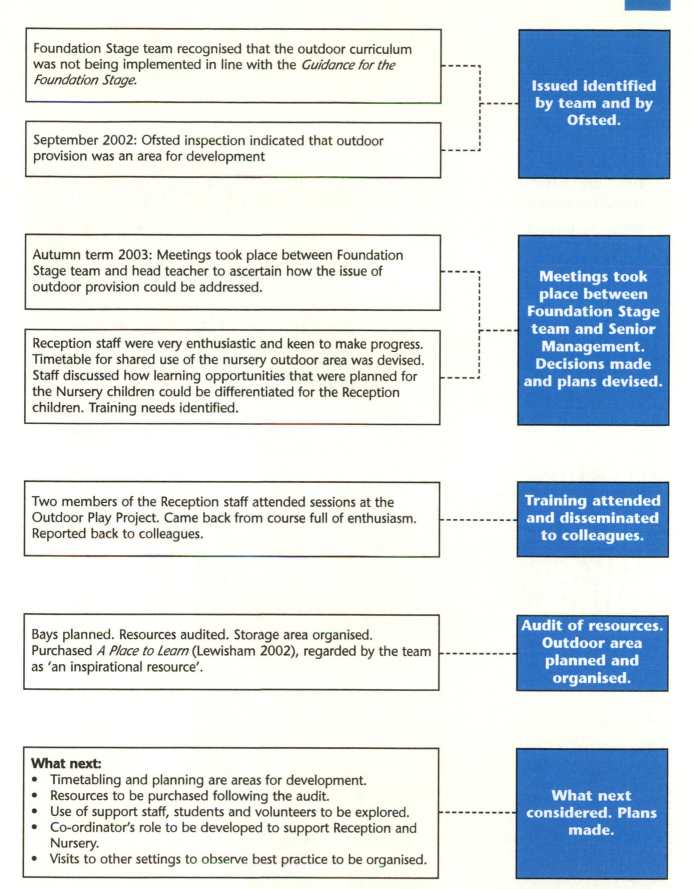

Foundation Stage team recognised that the outdoor curriculum was not being implemented in line with the *Guidance for the Foundation Stage.*

September 2002: Ofsted inspection indicated that outdoor provision was an area for development

Issued identified by team and by Ofsted.

Autumn term 2003: Meetings took place between Foundation Stage team and head teacher to ascertain how the issue of outdoor provision could be addressed.

Reception staff were very enthusiastic and keen to make progress. Timetable for shared use of the nursery outdoor area was devised. Staff discussed how learning opportunities that were planned for the Nursery children could be differentiated for the Reception children. Training needs identified.

Meetings took place between Foundation Stage team and Senior Management. Decisions made and plans devised.

Two members of the Reception staff attended sessions at the Outdoor Play Project. Came back from course full of enthusiasm. Reported back to colleagues.

Training attended and disseminated to colleagues.

Bays planned. Resources audited. Storage area organised. Purchased *A Place to Learn* (Lewisham 2002), regarded by the team as 'an inspirational resource'.

Audit of resources. Outdoor area planned and organised.

What next:
- Timetabling and planning are areas for development.
- Resources to be purchased following the audit.
- Use of support staff, students and volunteers to be explored.
- Co-ordinator's role to be developed to support Reception and Nursery.
- Visits to other settings to observe best practice to be organised.

What next considered. Plans made.

Figure 1.8 A snapshot of events leading to development

3. Make a diagram of outdoor area and list the current resources.

4. Allocate position of bays – consider the natural layout of the land and make best use of fences, walls and quiet areas.

5. Make a list of the additional resources that are needed for each area – including recycled or 'found' objects.

6. Write to local shops, businesses and parents to ask them to collect or donate recycled or 'found' items.

7. Collect resources and store in boxes or on trolleys.

8. Organise bays, ensuring that the resources are accessible to the children (Figures 1.9 and 1.10).

Figure 1.9 Using a gate and a trolley to provide a mark-making area

Figure 1.10 A line of flower pots, a wheel barrow and a large tub of earth creates the beginning of a simple growing and exploration area

Developing the imaginative play area

Context

This Nursery School catering for children aged 3 to 5 on a full- and part-time basis already had a well-developed outdoor area. However, the staff felt that it needed an added focus to rekindle the interests of the children and the staff.

What happened

After attending training, the practitioner went back to her setting and shared the information in a staff meeting.

Initially it was decided that the focus for development was to make resource boxes around themes or different aspects of weather. However, after some consideration and discussion with colleagues the lead person for the project decided to develop the imaginative aspect of the bike play.

A staff meeting was called to share thoughts and expertise on 'The mechanics workshop'.

1. First the practitioners thought about the procedures involved in a visit to a local mechanic – booking an appointment, giving details of the vehicle and the problems experienced, handing over keys, and making arrangements to collect the vehicle and pay.

2. Ideas were recorded on flipcharts.

3. They listed the resources required for each of the processes, noting the additional requirements.

4. The list was displayed on the notice board to inform parents of the planned experience and to indicate the equipment and resources still needed.

5. Parents, practitioners and children visited the local mechanic's workshop.

6. Photographs were taken to remind the children of their visit.

7. The photographs were displayed on a board and the children discussed what they had seen and done.

8. Meanwhile, parents and practitioners were making collections of the resources still needed.

9. The children and practitioners then began to set up the mechanic's workshop area. They organised the following:
   - A reception area with telephone, appointment book, receipt book and till.
   - A waiting area with coffee-making facilities.
   - Clipboards to be available with checklists for 'mechanics' to complete when carrying out a 'service' or MOT.
   - Posters of car parts and tools were displayed on the wall, as was a calendar.
   - A couple of 'Haynes Car Manuals' as reference books for the 'mechanics'.
   - A workshop area was sectioned off with warning signs displayed.
   - Boxes of tools and planks of wood to make ramps were strategically placed and gloves were made available.

10. The practitioners worked in the mechanic's workshop, with the children, alternating roles between a mechanic and a dissatisfied customer.

2 Planning and resourcing outdoor play

This chapter describes how good practice in outdoor provision can be planned for, resourced and nurtured. The following factors all influence provision and attitude:

- Structuring your outdoor learning project
- Action plans and development plans
- Involving colleagues
- Including children in the process
- Resourcing the outdoor area
- Support from the early years advisory team
- Involving the community
- Awareness of the adult role
- Understanding what children are learning outdoors.

Some of these factors are discussed below.

Action plans and development plans

> **Blank versions of the action plans shown here can be downloaded from the publisher's website: http://www.routledgeteachers.com. These can then be adapted to suit your own needs.**

First, examine your existing provision and draw up an action plan of how you want to develop it. Indicate on the plan the timescale, likely costs and who would be involved. Small, specific targets will be the most achievable and manageable. Most action plans drawn up for the Brent project showed that the initial priority was to provide equipment for outdoors, such as setting up resource boxes. Among the key issues arising were:

- Developing free-flow indoor/outdoor play
- Developing bays in the outdoor area
- Designing storage spaces
- Tackling gender issues
- Developing imaginative play.

The following are specific examples of different types of action and development plans you can use. You can use a mixture of these if necessary.

'What? Why? How?' plans

One nursery manager wanted to improve access and storage of resources. She decided to purchase a shed as the first step. Her action plan is outlined in Figure 2.1.

What do you want to develop?	Why?	How?	Resources and cost	Who does what?	How long?	Evaluation and evidence
Organised resources that are accessible to staff and children, to increase their independence	So that the outdoor play runs more smoothly and efficiently. Resources more accessible	By organising the existing storage areas and providing additional storage	Clear boxes with lids to store equipment Purchase shed from DIY store (up to £100)	Staff to organise existing resources Manager to buy shed	3 months	Lists of resources
Collect more resources for outdoors to offer wider choice and variety	So children develop a variety of skills and can explore	By offering children more learning opportunities	Compost, moss, piping, tubes and ropes	Manager and deputy to buy resources	6 months	Observations

Figure 2.1 Action Plan to develop storage and resources

Target	Action	Person responsible	Monitoring	Success criteria	Targets
What do we want to improve?	*What are we going to do?*	*Who is going to do it?*	*Who is going to check it is done?*	*How will we know if we have made a difference?*	*When are we going to do it by? (include review date)*
Supply clothing	**Collect together suitable clothing** for staff and children to wear outside	A	B	Children and staff suitably dressed for wet and cold weather Children have access to indoor and outdoor play what ever the weather	Oct 03 (Completed)
Resource bays	**Set up bays** Imaginative play Construction and building Large motor skills/gymnasium area Environmental and scientific Garden area Quiet area Small apparatus	A & B	B	Children use resources outside that they would not use inside Parents and local community contributing to resourcing area	Nov 03 (Completed end of Nov)

Figure 2.2 Action plan for nursery outdoor area

'Target/action' plans

In another example (Figure 2.2) a private nursery used a different format for their action plan. This one involved the whole team. It shows their overall vision for their outdoor area. The short-term aims were to provide appropriate clothing before developing each learning bay and then consider planning, assessment for learning and how to involve parents.

Timelines

The timeline in Figure 2.3 was drawn up for seven months. It indicates how the practitioner would achieve two priorities from the action plan: to develop a wildlife area, and to create an outdoor drawing area. Like others, she realised that the outdoor area would not come together overnight: it takes time, funds and imagination, patience and perseverance.

September	■ Attended course on outdoor provision ■ Refined preliminary action plan
October	■ Discussed plan with childcare manager and staff ■ Suitability of wildlife area established ■ Contacted RSPB and Garden Centre ■ Cost, labour, etc. agreed
November	■ Written permission for photographs obtained from parents ■ Phoned recycling centre for resources ■ Phoned Children's Information Service for information regarding health and safety
December	■ Work began on preparing garden, digging areas ■ Contacted local tradesman about fitting outdoor chalkboard
January	■ Obtained clay to make bird bath ■ Started to dig holes for shrubs
February	■ Visited garden centre to choose plants, etc. ■ Selected suitable pond
March	■ Bought shrubs and planted in garden ■ Fitted outdoor chalkboard

Figure 2.3 Timeline for developing priorities from the action plan

Floor plans

It is helpful to draw a plan of the outdoor area to illustrate the permanent features in your outdoor provision and where there are opportunities for change.

> Reviewing the current features in your outdoor area may enable you to be conscious of and value the potential learning opportunities that already exist for the children. Seemingly mundane features can often reveal new potential if interpreted with some imagination and meaning. (Learning Through Landscapes undated: 3)

Modifying action plans to suit your needs

Some action plans highlight how existing features might be used in imaginative ways. In one case, an underused climbing frame was commissioned as a role-play area, and in another a fenced-off garden was destined to become a digging patch. Later, over-ambitious action plans were modified to take account of practicalities.

A nursery teacher drew up a diagram of her outdoor area (Figure 2.4) and then made a timeline for a year, which helped to organise the way in which the outdoor area at her setting would be developed (Figure 2.5). For each area she drew up a mini action plan, which showed the key action points (Figure 2.6).

Sept–Nov	Dec–Feb	Mar–May	June–July
Set up bike track (Area 1)	Set up painting area (Area 2)	Set up stage (Area 3)	Set up throwing area (Area 4)

Figure 2.5 Year's timeline to allocate priorities

Why?	**Give reasons why this area is important to children's development**
	The outdoor environment provides a rich context for role-play. There is enough space to make role-play believable outdoors.
How?	**What will you do first?**
	Develop a stage area with secure wooden staging.
Where?	**Are there any special considerations?**
	Does it need to be near a particular resource – water, shed?
	Position in an area where noise is acceptable and children can move freely.
Resources?	**What would be the most important things to collect?**
	Pallet, curtains, microphone, pieces of fabric for dressing up, mark-making materials for children to make signs, tickets, etc.
Who?	**Will it be the team's responsibility or will someone else be involved?**
	Head teacher/manager to make bid for grant
	Caretaker and parents involved in assembling area
Success criteria?	**What will the children be doing?**
	Accessing the area frequently
	Using the area for extended periods
	Including other children as an audience
	Linking with learning taking place indoors

Figure 2.6 A mini action plan to set up the stage area

A few months into the project, two nursery nurses, supported by an advisory teacher, analysed the strengths and weaknesses of their outdoor area (see the Individual Educator Audit checklist at www.fultonpublishers.co.uk). This helped to clarify where the hold-ups occurred and also identified how the access to some equipment could be improved.

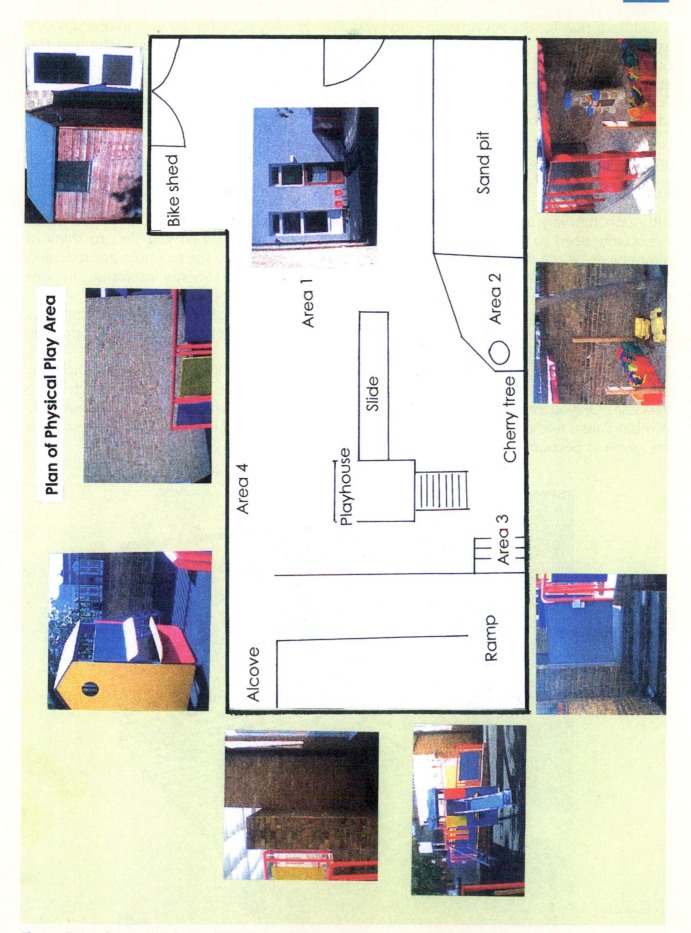

Figure 2.4 A diagram of the outdoor area, indicating areas for development

Outdoor play for the Foundation Stage was already a key issue for the year in one school's improvement plan. The whole-school target was to improve learning and teaching in the outdoor curriculum through an audit of equipment, weekly planning for outdoor learning and staff training. This contributed to the performance management targets for the Foundation Stage Co-ordinator, whose role it was to monitor the learning and teaching taking place outdoors.

Resourcing the outdoor area

Funding issues

Although funding is important, financial restrictions need not be prohibitive. You don't necessarily need to purchase large, purpose-built equipment. When you start to think of alternatives, you'll find there are almost unlimited possibilities, for example approaching local shops for large boxes or a bus station for extra-large tyres. Some interesting images can be obtained via the Internet, printed off and laminated for display.

Begin to collect resources by making requests to members of staff, parents, companies and local stores. Rummaging through sheds and cupboards has been known to provide enough paint to begin to transform one outdoor area.

Knowing what to get and avoiding expensive mistakes is important. Avoid choosing equipment, in particular climbing frames, that is too restrictive. A-frames are much more versatile. Or you can use freely available resources to create exciting and manoeuvrable climbing areas and obstacle courses (Figure 2.7). Suggestions of ways to use these resources are given in Section 3B.

Figure 2.7 Creating an obstacle course

Tyres

Tyres are great for climbing, and the children can be involved in scrubbing them clean and rolling them into position (Figure 2.8). They can also be made into obstacle courses or bike tracks that the children can alter.

Using builders' trays

You can create a mini world using beads, lentils and stones in a builders' tray, which offers children rich opportunities to use their imaginations (Figure 2.9).

'Don't be afraid to beg, steal or borrow. Searching skips and asking if goods are finished with are good ways to resource the outdoor area,' is the advice given by one team.

Figure 2.8 Recycling old tyres

Figure 2.9 Making a face with assorted materials in a builders' tray

Clothing and wellington boots

You can ask parents to bring in wellington boots and warm, waterproof clothing for outdoor play or acquire sets of protective clothing, boots and umbrellas that can be shared or borrowed. Having the right clothing gives the children much more freedom.

During the summer months, sun hats and sun cream are equally important considerations.

Underused resources

During the project, unused resources were discovered (Figures 2.10 and 2.11).

Figure 2.10 A fascination with CDs

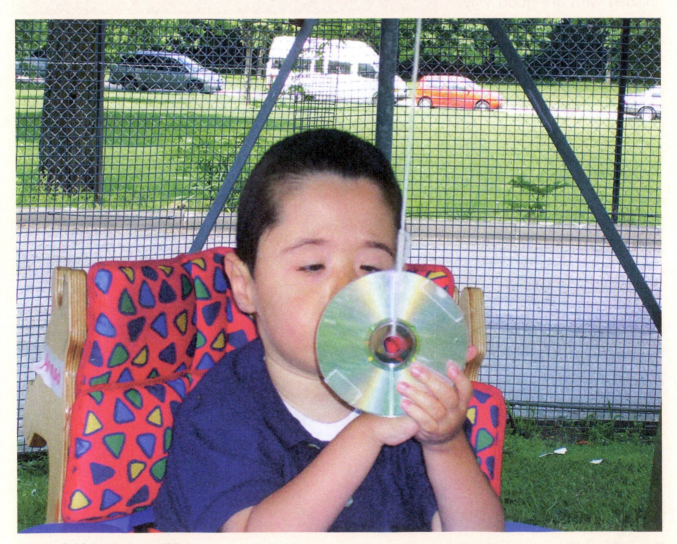

Figure 2.11 Exploring a CD

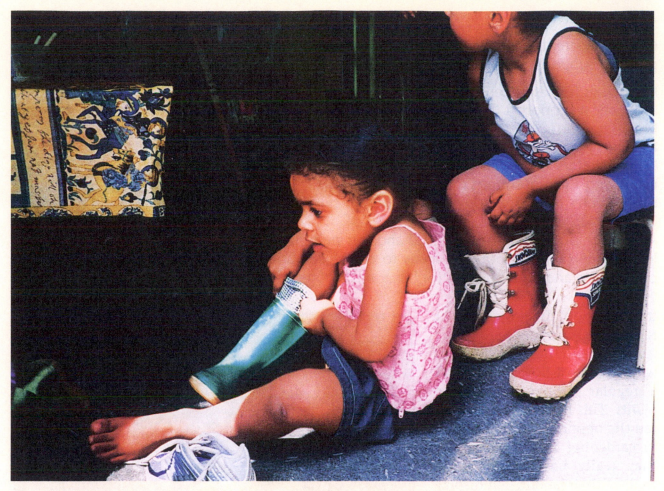

Figure 2.12 Wellington boots enable children to go out in all weathers

Organising and storing equipment

For many, a shed or trolley is essential to make outdoor play manageable. The additional burden for staff of setting up another learning environment can be offset by good-quality storage facilities. Where staff have high expectations of children, the children became more independent (Figures 2.13 and 2.14) and staff are freed to interact with children rather than supervise. When children can find the correct storage box easily, this will make the task of providing equipment outdoors speedy and efficient.

Involving the community

Make use of available advice and practical help from as many sources as possible, including:

- Trades people
- Community
- Families
- Parents.

Access to skilled workers eases the burden on time and resources and leads to more rapid progress. Additionally, carpenters and plumbers who are already associated with the setting have been known to supply free resources and be helpful in setting up the outdoor learning environment.

Involving parents

Crucially, parents need to be involved in developing outdoor provision. You can engage parental support in a number of ways, including:

- Appeals for resources
- Practical support
- Fundraising
- Raising awareness of the importance of outdoor play
- Newsletters
- Sharing their intentions for learning outdoors
- Children's responses to outdoor play.

Asking for practical support and 'hands-on help' is often very successful. Parents can be involved in painting outdoor areas to create colourful seating, making markings on the playground and parking areas for bikes and scooters. Here are a few examples.

In a preschool the project leader reported, 'One of our parents is a gardener and has provided us with dozens of flower bulbs and a regular supply of bedding plants. This has given the children the opportunity to take part in gardening and planting and they really have enjoyed the fruits of their labour. Our display of spring flowers was also quite spectacular!'

A community nursery invited parents and carers to an outdoor fun week, declaring that it was combining opportunities to 'help revitalise the garden for your children with your children' and to fundraise. They opened a food stall to raise funds for outdoor equipment and involved parents in a range of developments in the outdoor area. These ideas included developing a vegetable patch, dens and shelters, a musical tree, a magnetic board and an insect garden. The result of this was a good deal of interest and enthusiasm from the parent volunteers, an action plan for the nursery and a much improved outdoor area.

To raise parental understanding of the importance of

Figure 2.13 Helping to tidy up by sweeping up with a broom

Figure 2.14 Confidently returning two cones to the shed

outdoor play, the principal of a Montessori nursery shared a memorable quote from the outdoor conference with the parents in her setting via a newsletter: 'The longer you keep children sitting, the less attentive they become. Increasing time spent on adult directed tasks at the expense of play produces many early signs of ADHD, especially in boys' (Pellegrini 1998).

She followed this with Sally Goddard-Blyth's comment (2000) that 'children who are unable to sit still or pay attention need more time engaged in physical activities'. In the newsletter, the principal summarised why outdoor play is essential and gave an overview of how it would be incorporated into the daily life of the nursery. Parents were asked to work with the nursery by putting an extra layer of clothing on their child and expecting that the children may come home a little muddy occasionally.

Figure 2.15 Talking about a recent discovery

Figure 2.16 Taking time to listen

Displaying photographs and sending letters enhances parental understanding of outdoor play. Parents hear about the children playing outside, listen to their children talking about their outdoor learning and so become aware of its positive effects. Some settings share their planning with parents to demonstrate what children learn in the outdoor environment.

However, the most influential factor is the delight of the children themselves. Where children are 'dragging' parents in to see the nursery garden and talking about the excitement of learning outdoors, parents too find it hard to resist the lure of outdoor play. When parents come to collect children at nursery they might be greeted by children saying, 'See what we've done', and they began to discover what learning has taken place that day.

Figure 2.17 Sometimes the adult is guiding the child, sometimes having fun and talking to the child

' **My child looks forward to coming to nursery because she loves the outdoor area. We don't have a garden at home so the nursery garden is really important to her.** '

' **I thought outdoor play was just about riding bikes but they're all busy doing things. It's really good.** '

For many parents, regardless of cultural and philosophical differences, outdoor play makes a real difference to the quality of their children's lives, and they are enthusiastic once their initial anxieties have been allayed. Parents are delighted that their children are so keen to come to nursery and that they are happy when they play outside. Fostering positive parental attitudes to outdoor learning is demanding, but essential.

The adult's role

Be confident. Your role is of crucial importance if the children are really to benefit from outdoor play. When starting to develop the outdoor area, many people feel that equipment is a priority, but actually it's you who holds the key. If you are enthusiastic, provide exciting outdoor experiences and have a clear understanding of what you want to promote, children's learning does flourish. Learn when to stand back and when to intervene and at what level. Sometimes this is literal, for example crouching at the child's level when looking at things on the ground (Figure 2.15). Respond sensitively to develop children's confidence.

Changes in staff attitudes

'Time spent outdoors encourages practitioners to interact with children outside, not as supervisors but as educators' (Ouvry 2000: 22).

One of the aims of the project was to increase practitioners' confidence in providing outdoor play, so to see such engagement was rewarding (Figures 2.16 and 2.17).

Prioritise children's learning as your main reason for promoting outdoor play. Planning for both indoor and outdoor environments so that each is of equal value leads to focused activities being introduced outdoors. It is not just setting up the environment, but planning and thinking about how children learn in a holistic way. Appreciate that children are drawn outside because of the freedom and excitement it brings to them.

One outdoor project leader held this view: 'Indoors we are on top of children; outdoors we are following them.' She urged her staff to look for opportunities for learning and exploring as they observed, listened and shared ideas about what children were doing outdoors. She concluded by telling them, 'The responsibility for good, meaningful outdoor activities clearly lies with the adults.' The outdoors should be well organised and planned, prepared as a haven for learning.

'There's something for everyone to do outside.'

'Children seem bright and alert outside. It's as though it wakes them up.'

'They are well contented.'

'They're calmer and will approach activities and be more focused.'

'Children can just exist – no pressures from adults.'

'Be a child yourself again and join in the fun. We do.'

'Looking through a child's eyes heightens awareness of the potential of learning outdoors.'

3 Creating the outdoor learning environment

Figure 3.1 Drumming

In this chapter we explore the way in which the outdoor learning environment is organised and give examples of learning opportunities and resources.

Bays

The outdoor environment, like the indoor environment, should be organised into resource-based learning bays. This can be done on a permanent basis, or, if space is limited, resources can be stored on trolleys, which can be wheeled into place as required. The learning bays are resourced in such a way that children can access the resources and equipment in them independently. 'Young children are only just finding out where to find things, e.g. scissors, bats, balls, etc. If they have to keep relearning where to go and where things are, it wastes their energy' (Bruce and Meggit 1996: 372). Wherever possible, the materials in these bays should be available all day every day. When similar resources are grouped together they can have a positive effect on children's learning. Equally, children need to feel that the resources can be used flexibly and that they can combine them within and between the different bays.

Bilton (2004: 40) suggests organising resources by developing these bays:

- Imaginative play
- Building and construction
- Gymnasium
- Small apparatus
- Horticultural
- Environmental and scientific
- Art
- Quiet.

Whereas Edgington (2003: 12) suggests the following:

- Climbing area
- Space to run
- Wheeled-vehicle area
- Space to develop skills with small equipment
- Quiet area
- Places to hide
- Wild area
- An area for large-scale construction and imaginative play
- Space for play with natural materials
- A gardening area.

These ideas have been combined to produce the following list, which is described in more detail in the basic resource list later in this chapter (see pages 29–43).

- **Creative area.** This might include weaving, painting, sand, water, mark-making and music making.
- **Quiet area.** This might include books and a 'space to be'.
- **Imaginative play area.** This might include building and construction.
- **Environmental area.** This might include digging, growing and wild area.
- **An open space.** This could be used flexibly and could be somewhere that children could:
  a. Use small equipment such as balls, bean bags, hoops
  b. Run
  c. Ride wheeled vehicles
  d. Climb or balance.

A predictable environment is essential. Children need to know where the resources will be stored in order for them to gain access when items are needed. Trolleys or sets of drawers are extremely useful for this purpose (Figures 3.2, 3.3 and 3.4). They can be wheeled into location at the beginning of each day and stored at the end of the day. Labelling the tubs or drawers in the trolley will enable staff and children to find what they need and return it after use. The most effective labels are those drawn/written by the children or photographs of the children using the resources. These are meaningful and are 'owned' by the children. This strategy also enables children to learn where everything is kept and will make tidying-up a learning opportunity. Number labels can be used to identify how many of each item there should be. This also helps to maintain the stock of resources.

Figure 3.2 Storing good quality resources outdoors

Figure 3.3 A trolley keeps everything that is needed to hand

In some nurseries the trolley/storage box is placed in the appropriate bay at the beginning of the day, and in others children take the responsibility for setting out the equipment as their interests dictate. Alternatively, the outdoor space can permanently set up with additional resources added as indicated by children's interests.

When deciding where to place the bays, you should also consider boundaries. These create important divisions and provide a focus for the different experiences that are being offered. They can also ensure privacy and provide a safe route between bays (Figures 3.5 and 3.6).

Figure 3.4 Using a mini-greenhouse for storing art materials

Suggestions for the learning bays

The pages that follow suggest what to put in each of the five areas described above and what learning opportunities might be possible.

In each area it might be useful to consider how ICT can be used as a tool to promote effective learning outdoors (Section 3D).

The suggestion pages are organised into three sections:

- ■ The first gives a flavour of the opportunities for learning that may occur in each bay.
- ■ The second provides ideas about the type of displays that could be organised in each bay. If you have to pack everything away at the end of the day you can attach posters or photographs onto metal coat hangers and hook these onto fences, down pipes, or hang them on masonry nails hammered into the buildings. This is a quick and easy way to transform the environment and inspire children's work.
- ■ The final section contains suggestions of the resources or pieces of equipment that 'live' in the bay. It is important to ensure that these resources complement, extend or are completely different from those provided indoors. This list is not exhaustive, but serves as a checklist of basic provision for a stimulating outdoor environment.

Figure 3.5 Bays need boundaries

Figure 3.6 A mini-beast area with a boundary

CREATIVE AREA

This area might include space for painting, weaving, sand and water, mark-making and provision for music-making.

PAINTING

Opportunity

- To create large-scale painting on large sheets of wallpaper, on cloth on walls, on fences or on the ground
- To make rubbings of the different textures within the environment, for example of tree trunks, paving, manhole covers, brick walls, grills
- To experiment freely with resources and image
- To work together and independently

Display

- Laminated prints of artists' works from a range of cultures
- Pictures of people's faces, across all ethnic groups
- Laminated pictures of landscapes from all over the world
- An outdoor exhibition of children's creative work

Basic resources

- Paint: ready-made in squeezy bottles or powder paint ready to make
- Trolley containing pots of large brushes of varying widths and sizes
- A selection of tools to apply paint: palette knives, spatulas, sponges, mini-mops, sticks
- A rack containing a variety of large sheets of paper of different colours, textures, sizes, lengths and shapes
- Sheets of greaseproof paper, tin foil, newspaper
- Drying rack or line that children can use independently
- Pencils for children to write their names
- Lengths of cloth/plastic sheeting attached to the fence for group painting experiences

Figure 3.7 Boys painting a wall with big buckets and brushes

WEAVING

Opportunity

- To design and contribute to the weaving wall
- To create a wall hanging
- To make pictures or patterns with petals, leaves, twig, bark, shells or stones

Display

- Books and posters to stimulate interest
- Laminated pictures of weavings or wall hangings or tapestry
- Invitations to create a range of weavings, etc.

Basic resources

- Selection of materials in baskets or on a trolley: strips of paper, lengths of ribbon, feathers, lengths of fabric, lengths of willow, sheets of cellophane, cut-up strips made from plastic bags, sequin strips
- Bark, leaves, wool, wood shavings
- Masking tape, elastic bands, string, split pins, paper clips
- Twigs and lengths of rope

Figure 3.8 Weaving – working together on a large-scale creation

SAND, GRAVEL, BARK CHIPPINGS OR SMALL PEBBLES

Opportunity

- To dig in or sit in a deep container and select equipment to use in the sand from a variety placed in a large basket
- A beach area can be developed by placing sand on large sheets of plastic or tarpaulin

Display

- Laminated pictures of sand in its natural form
- Rules for the number of children allowed to use the sand at any one time and other rules devised with children

Basic resources

- Deep sand container or loose sand in an enclosed area
- Sand hats
- Basket for sand equipment
- Large spades and buckets
- Short-handled stiff broom for children to sweep up after themselves
- Large stones or pebbles
- Shells or pine cones
- Cover for sand

Figure 3.9 Sitting in the sand working alongside one another

WATER

Opportunity

- To explore running water and discover how water moves and changes, without worrying about spillages
- To experience rain and puddles
- To look at frozen water, for example frost, ice, snow
- To make trails or to experiment with forces and trajectories

Figure 3.10 An opportunity to experience moving water

Display

- Laminated pictures of running water in its various forms
- Laminated pictures of dams or piping systems
- Laminated pictures of children/adults splashing in the rain or sheltering under umbrellas

Basic resources

- Containers at various heights to enable water to flow
- An outside tap or a water butt with tap and hose attachment
- Aprons
- Lengths of guttering, lengths of plastic and copper pipe, buckets, jugs, funnels, plastic tubing, pots and pans
- Wellington boots, umbrellas, raincoats or splash suits
- Squeezy bottles filled with water
- Food colouring, bottles and cauldrons to make potions and spells, large wooden and metal spoons, sticks to stir with

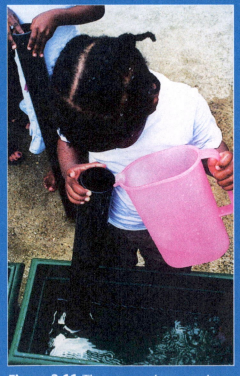

Figure 3.11 Time to explore moving water and attempt to control its flow

Figure 3.12 Guttering creates new learning opportunities when attached to a fence

MUSIC

Opportunity

- To explore natural sounds within the environment
- To make loud music and compose collaboratively
- To dance or perform for themselves or an impromptu audience
- To dance to taped music
- To dance or perform on a low stage made from wooden pallets

Display

- Laminated pictures of people playing a variety of instruments, for example African drums, percussion instruments
- Laminated pictures of dancers from a range of cultures, for example ballet, hip hop, ballroom, Latin American, rock and roll, hobnail boot dancers, Irish dancers

Basic resources

- Metal oil drums, plastic oil drums, metal saucepans hanging from a fence, lengths of copper piping, tin lids, metal rubbish bin lid, bells
- Beaters made from metal, plastic or wood
- Tape recorder (with microphone), echo mike, karaoke machine, radio mikes
- Bottles filled with water or other materials which change the sounds made
- CD player or tape recorder with variety of music from different cultures and styles
- Ankle and wrist bells
- Swathes of cloth and dressing-up clothes
- Mirrors to observe own dancing

Figure 3.13 Musical clothes horse

Figure 3.14 Hanging bottles make interesting sounds

Figure 3.15 Large xylophone

QUIET AREA

This area might include a book area and a quiet place 'to be'.

BOOK/QUIET AREA

Opportunity

- To refer to books and find information about a creature they have found
- To share stories with friends or an adult or look at books independently
- To escape from the 'watchful eye' of adults into dens and hidey holes

Display

- Laminated posters of readers from a variety of ethnic/minority groups, including children with disabilities
- Invitations to share a book
- Attention drawn to writers and illustrators from a range of cultures
- Storyboards and props in a variety of languages

Basic resources

- Books organised into small easily reached baskets, for example organised into fiction/reference, colour-coded for tidying up
- Variety of books including dual language, picture books, traditional books, books that reflect the diversity of our society (lifestyle, culture, ability), home-made books
- Reference books on mini-beasts, flowers, plants and vegetation
- Cushions, carpet squares
- Small table
- Battery-operated tape recorder/CD player, Dictaphone
- Tapes and CDs of songs, stories
- Tents

Figure 3.16 A quiet place to be

Figure 3.17 A piece of tarpaulin can create a quiet, dark space

IMAGINATIVE AREA

This area would contain opportunities for imaginative play and the building and construction area.

IMAGINATIVE PLAY

Opportunity

- To set their own play agenda and explore the open-ended props that are available
- To act out stories or real-life situations, for example:
  - Garage or mechanics
  - Ambulance, police or fire stations
  - Removal vans
  - Car washes
  - Fast-food cafes, drive-throughs and delivery services
  - Flower delivery
  - Roadside rescue services
  - Building sites
  - Bus station, railway station, airport
  - Farms
  - Garden centres
  - Market stalls
  - Picnic area
  - Ice cream van
  - Dispatch rider
  - Builder/plasterer
  - Window cleaner

Display

- Laminated photographs of children in role
- Books and laminated photographs relating to each idea
- Washing line to hang drapes on
- Stands or clothes airers

Basic resources

- A-frames and lengths of cloth
- Large cardboard boxes, plastic crates
- Plastic sheeting, tarpaulin, heavy pieces of material, curtains or long lengths of floaty, shiny cloth
- Tree-trunk sections, large logs and pine cones
- Tents, tables and boxes
- Pallet for a stage with shower curtain attached
- Hose pipe cut to lengths or washing machine hoses for fire fighters
- Lengths of rope, pegs, masking tape

- Broom handles with 'traffic lights' (a broom handle dropped into a large cone or cemented into a bucket)
- Writing resources, including pads and pencils, clipboards
- Telephone and directory
- Dressing-up materials, for example capes, masks and wraps
- Selection of bags, purses, hats and shoes
- Maps and rucksacks, sleeping bags, picnic set and blanket, baskets, suitcases
- Builder's belt, mallets, screwdrivers, spirit levels, pulleys
- Walkie-talkies

Figure 3.18 Planks of wood make great ramps

Figure 3.19 Building with crates

ENVIRONMENTAL AREA

This could include a digging area, a growing area and a wild area in which children can explore and discover what's around them.

ENVIRONMENTAL

Opportunity

- ■ To discover the wonders of the immediate environment
- ■ To engage in scientific enquiry
- ■ To learn about caring for the environment
- ■ To appreciate the changing seasons

Display

- ■ Laminated pictures of spider webs, leaves, trees, mini-beasts, etc.
- ■ Reference books linked to the area of discovery that the children are currently interested in

Basic resources

- ■ Trees to climb, shrubs and plants
- ■ Magnifying glasses, plastic mirrors, large magnets
- ■ Bug boxes, margarine tubs, hand lenses
- ■ Digging equipment, gloves, trowels
- ■ Carpet tiles to kneel on
- ■ Carpet tiles to place in a damp area to attract mini-beasts
- ■ Clipboards with paper and pencils
- ■ Willow sculptures or archways
- ■ Digital camera to record findings

Figure 3.20 Piling logs safely adds another dimension for children to explore

WILD AREA

Opportunity

■ To investigate flora and fauna in their natural habitat

Display

■ Laminated cards or pictures that help children to identify the organisms found in the local environment

Basic resources

■ Overgrown area – sown with 'meadow' flowers
■ Bird table and feeder
■ Plants that attract wildlife, for example buddleia, nettles, clover, honeysuckle
■ Pond (old water tray) covered with a grill and filled with water plants
■ Highly scented plants, for example rosemary, thyme, lemon balm, lavender, curry plant, tobacco plant, lovage, mint
■ Logs, rocks and old bricks

DIGGING AREA

Opportunity

■ To dig in the mud and investigate their findings
■ To investigate the properties of soil, both wet and dry

Display

■ Photos of diggers or people digging

Basic resources

■ Digging equipment, including shovels, forks, spades
■ Gloves, specimen boxes, lolly sticks
■ Logs, over-grown foliage
■ Carpet tiles on which to kneel
■ Upside-down flower pots
■ Metal detectors

Figure 3.21 Converting an old bookcase to make a digging area

Figure 3.22 Providing the right clothes is essential

Figure 3.23 Digging area

GROWING AREA

Opportunity

- To grow plants, herbs and flowers
- To plant bulbs and seeds
- To plant, tend and care for living things
- To eat home-grown produce, for example fruits, vegetables and herbs
- To record the life-cycle of the plants and chart the way they change and develop

Display

Laminated sheets inviting children to carry out activities, for example:

- Look closely at the bulb. What do you think it will grow into?
- Make a label for your plant.
- Draw a picture of what your plant will look like when it has grown.

Basic resources

- Grow bags, planters, plots of earth
- Gardening tools including spades, trowels, forks, gardening gloves, wheelbarrows, watering cans, hoses, canes
- Seeds, bulbs, plants
- Writing and drawing materials

Figure 3.24 Planting in tyres

Figure 3.25 Learning to use a wheelbarrow

OPEN SPACE AREA

This could be adapted as required into an area to run, an area to climb and balance, or an area in which to use small equipment such as balls, beanbags and hoops.

GYMNASIUM

Opportunity

■ To balance, gain spatial awareness and first-hand experience of being upside down, on top of something or inside something
■ To develop body strength by pulling, pushing, rolling and lifting pieces of equipment

Display

■ Arrows or signs to create obstacle courses

Basic resources

■ Planks, A-frames, poles, ladders, hoops
■ Boxes, crates, barrels, tunnels, off-cuts of huge pipes
■ Beams, logs, tyres, cones, canes, ropes
■ Cubes, triangular boxes
■ Climbing walls

Figure 3.26 An outdoor gymnasium

Figure 3.28 Using logs to develop a game

Figure 3.27 Using found materials to create an obstacle course

SMALL APPARATUS

Opportunity

■ To develop skills such as throwing, retrieving, catching, aiming, rolling, bowling, kicking, batting

Figure 3.29 Children need space to play with bats and balls

Display

■ Famous sports people
■ Targets marked on walls or fences

Basic resources

■ Beanbags, balls of various sizes, weights and materials
■ Quoits, bats, hoops of various sizes
■ Large dice
■ Plastic bottles filled with coloured water to be used as skittles
■ Streamers, long ribbons, pom-poms
■ Stilts
■ Squeezy bottles filled with water that can be aimed at targets (e.g. holes made in cardboard boxes)
■ Targets made from wire coat hangers hung above head height or buckets or hoops
■ Easel to record scores
■ Tights hung on a line with sponge balls, leaves or towelling in the toes

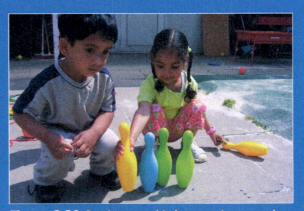

Figure 3.30 Setting up skittles requires good co-ordination

Figure 3.31 Rolling balls through tubes into a tyre

WHEELED VEHICLES

Opportunity

- To experience speed and negotiate pathways
- To co-operate with others
- To engage in role play
- To develop large muscle groups

Display

- Laminated numbers, number plates and road signs
- Traffic lights on broom handles stuck in buckets of concrete
- Zebra crossings
- Photos of petrol stations or emergency services

Basic resources

- Wheeled vehicles to push and pull such as wagons, chariots, two-person bikes, carts, wheelbarrows
- Two- and three-wheeler bikes with number plates
- Supermarket trolley, sturdy push chair
- Plastic road cones, road signs
- Numbered parking bays
- Remote control cars
- Maps and tool boxes

Conclusion

In this chapter we have offered our interpretation of what a well-resourced outdoor area looks like and the experiences it can offer. Many items are inexpensive or home-made and will prompt children to use their imaginations. When challenged with open-ended opportunities 'children set themselves demanding tasks that challenge all their abilities' (Ouvry 2000: 34). Setting up outdoor bays in this way will facilitate children's independent learning. It places responsibility on everyone concerned, i.e. practitioners, children and parents, and will ensure that the learning opportunities outdoors are maximised.

4 What do children learn outdoors?

Introduction

Children learn with an enthusiasm and motivation outdoors that they do not always display indoors. From most children's point of view 'this is the place that they want to be', as the principal of a Montessori nursery put it. There is evidence that children who regularly have access to outdoor provision experience better health and their attendance is correspondingly better. Parents of some children reported that their children were coming home from nursery refreshed and not frustrated. This has had considerable benefit for the families, children and settings.

When children are given access on a free-flow basis to outdoor provision their confidence level rises. Is this because they have:

- A wider range of learning opportunities outdoors?
- Open-ended resources?
- Opportunity to work with 'the stuff of the earth'?
- More time to follow through their ideas and return to them day after day?
- More open space so they do not feel constantly under the watchful eye of adults?
- Opportunities to follow their own interests and ideas and create their own play agenda?
- Opportunities to be more active, and work on a larger, messier and noisier scale than indoors?
- More responsibility for their own actions because the adults may not be so close by?
- So much to be excited and curious about in a constantly changing environment?
- More opportunities for communal activity?
- More opportunity to look after each other and assist with physical tasks?

This chapter gives examples of the deep-level learning that children can be involved in when they are given the opportunity to work in well resourced, stimulating outdoor environments. However, it should be noted that these examples do not cover all the learning that can take place outside. Rather they offer an insight into the development that took place in the settings over a year.

We have looked at children's learning under the following headings:

- Exploring and investigating
- Communication
- Being active, less inhibited and free
- Taking time out (reflecting)
- The Elements
- Construction
- Role play
- Art ephemera
- Higher-order thinking.

Exploring and investigating

Mini-beasts

Being outside offers children the opportunity to observe creatures in their natural environment. Children in the project settings began to respect the animals and mini-beasts that they found and this reduced their fear of these creatures.

In Figure 4.1 the children appear to be confidently observing a 'sleeping' snail. Figure 4.2 demonstrates how the adult can support children whose confidence wavers as the snail begins to move across the lid.

Figure 4.1 Children look closely at a snail

Figure 4.2 With adult support the children continued to watch the snail

At one particular nursery, opportunities for cross-curricular learning developed following a child's self-initiated exploration of the creatures that live in or under the pallets in the garden. The nursery's theme was mini-beasts; the children and adults went on a bug hunt and found some snails under one of the wooden pallets in the garden. The children observed the snails on the pallets, with some of the younger children being very cautious to begin with. One child noticed the snail trail and asked, 'What's that?' After a conversation with other children and the adult, the child was overheard commenting, 'It's shiny!'

The following day one of the children went into the garden and tried to lift a pallet in the imaginative area saying that she wanted to see, 'if there were bugs underneath'. With the support of an adult she discovered woodlice, earwigs and ants. Using her initiative, she went inside and found a reference book about mini-beasts. She found the page with the woodlice on and compared the picture with the real thing. During the conversation that followed, the child made comments about the sizes of the woodlice, using words such as 'small, baby one and big one'. She also took the magnifier to get a closer look at the wood louse and said, 'It has lots of legs. Look!'

Staff put the snails in a glass tank for a few days so that the children could feed them and observe them more closely. As a result of this, some children took clipboards, paper and pencils from the investigations box and made observational drawings of the snails.

Children are really motivated and excited about what they see in the outdoor environment. Just look at how engrossed this child is as she intently observes the behaviour of ants (Figure 4.3).

Figure 4.3 Closely observing ants

In time, children develop a greater awareness of the environment as they become totally engrossed in the lives, movements, habits and habitation of mini-beasts. Playing outdoors heightens children's interest in mini-beasts and they are less frightened when they encounter them outdoors: 'They are so small! It's going under the pot!' It's up to you to spend time supporting these young scientists.

In settings where there are animals, children gain huge benefits from contact with them. They learn to show care and responsibility. They also develop an awareness of different stages of life. 'Nothing awakens foresight in a small child, who lives as a rule for the passing moment and without a care for the morrow as taking care of plants and especially animals' (Montessori 1988: 73).

Through these experiences, children can:

■ Observe living creatures in their natural habitats
■ Respect living creatures

- Use reference books to gain more knowledge
- Develop the vocabulary of the 'here and now'
- Describe what is seen
- Use mathematical language in context
- Record what they see by making representational drawings.

Extending play over a period of time

Wellington boots, waterproof clothing, coats and gardening gloves enable children to engage in this type of play whatever the weather. The boys in Figure 4.4 were engaged in filling the buckets with stones and transferring them from one container to the other. They observed that water had collected under the stones and explored the creatures that were living there: 'I caught worms. There's water at the bottom of this (sandpit). We put it there last week from the well.' They collected larger stones from another area of the garden, which they arranged carefully and commented, 'The nest would be for the birds.'

The three boys were engrossed in their play and co-operated throughout this task, which lasted all morning. This play scenario had begun the previous week when the boys had noticed the water that had collected in the well and had transported some to the sandpit.

Through this experience, children can:

- Be motivated and engrossed in their play
- Be independent of adults
- Be able to continue a shared narrative from one week to the next
- Be free to work together at their own pace
- Be engaged in purposeful mathematical learning, 'children are more engaged in mathematical learning when combined with physical movement' (observation of a nursery practitioner)
- Experience weight.

Exploring water

In Figures 4.5 and 4.6 the children are investigating the marks that can be made with water. They have selected large rollers and are involved in pursuing their own interests by covering an area of the playground with water. Boys are more likely to become involved in mark-making activities when the resources enable them to create on the move.

Through this experience, children can:

- Be involved in mark-making
- Use large motor movements
- Create semi-permanent marks
- Learn about scientific concepts such as evaporation
- Explore mathematical concepts such as space and length
- Understand that tools are used for a specific purpose.

Figure 4.4 Co-operative play developed over a two-week period

Figure 4.5 Using large rollers to cover an area of ground with water

Figure 4.6 Mark-making with water

Figure 4.7 Experimenting with flowing water

A nursery wanted to extend children's experience of water. By fixing two lengths of guttering onto a piece of hardboard, attached to some railings children were encouraged to explore the properties of running water. An outside tap and a range of resources allowed them to be in control of their own learning. Over a period of weeks a child discovered which container created the best flow of water (Figures 4.7 and 4.8). He spent many hours using the tap to fill different sized containers and watched the results as he poured water into the guttering. With adult support, he came to realise that the more water he had, the faster it would flow.

Figure 4.8 Working together to catch the flow

Through this experience, children could:

■ Explore the properties of running water
■ Realise that water flows down a slope
■ Realise that pouring different quantities of water into the guttering affects the speed of the water
■ Experience how heavy jugs full of water are
■ Explore the scientific concepts of volume and capacity by using different sized and shaped jugs and buckets
■ Discuss what they are doing.

Bubbles

Children should be given the opportunity to explore different ways of making bubbles. Provide a variety of resources and give them the space (and trust) to investigate which substances make the best bubbles. Tennis rackets, funnels and rings can all provide good results but allow the children to experiment. Doing this outside makes it possible for the children to work in more depth because they are not constrained by the worry of making a mess. Over time, the children develop their own ideas about what can be used to make bubbles and whether the bubbles formed will be large or small.

Figure 4.9 Growing in troughs

Figure 4.10 Using the hose pipe to water the plants

Figure 4.11 Showing my twin sister a plant

Planting

Regardless of the make up of the outdoor environment, children can have the opportunity of planting either in pots or in the earth. There is no excuse! In Figures 4.9, 4.10 and 4.11 we can see children engaged in growing and caring for plants in various ways. In some settings that appear to be a tarmac desert where resources have to be cleared away at the end of each session, the potted plants will be the only things that are ever allowed to remain outside! The children can care for them daily and water them as needed.

Through this experience, children can:

■ Care for plants
■ Wonder at the 'miracle' of growth
■ Explore the various starting points of plants, for example pips, cuttings, seeds, bulbs, tubers
■ Observe and record change over time.

Communication

The outdoors is a rich environment that gives children 'More to talk about', and this develops the way that they communicate with each other and the adults around them, both through their body language and the written and verbal word. They spend more time thinking together, problem solving, negotiating, 'just being together', and relaxing in the company of others. Children with English as an additional language may speak more frequently. Once the nursery 'settles into' the idea and environments became better resourced and more challenging, children become very engaged and use the resources in a more purposeful way. The length of time that children are able to be outside has a direct correlation to the concentration levels they display and the type of activity they engage in.

Below are a few examples that show children using literacy in a purposeful way and doing things outside that they had not done inside.

Writing for a purpose

Some practitioners observed that boys were far more willing to write outdoors than they were indoors and that they demonstrated that they knew the purposes of literacy.

In Figure 4.12 we can see one boy enjoying writing for a purpose. He wanted to join other children dancing on the stage but was told that there was not enough room. His solution to this problem was to make a list with his name at the top, followed by names of other children (Figure 4.13). He used the list to gain his turn on the stage and inform the other children when it was their turn to dance and sing.

Figure 4.12 Writing his name at the top of the list

Figure 4.13 The other three children on the stage

Figure 4.14 Chalking on the ground

Figure 4.15 Chalking on the gate

Mark-making

Many opportunities for mark-making on a large scale were offered in the outdoor environment, and children were seen working alongside each other making comments about what they were doing (Figures 4.14 and 4.15).

> ' Boys become more confident writers outdoors and seem less inhibited and more willing to explore the various forms of mark-making. '

Through such experiences, children can:

- Explore different purposes for writing in context
- Access group play
- Work alongside others
- Use a variety of media and tools
- Gain control over large muscle groups
- Work comfortably at different levels.

Talking and co-operating – sharing ideas

The outside environment provides many opportunities for children to talk in animated ways, as seen in Figures 4.16, 4.17 and 4.18.

Figure 4.17 shows two children discussing their painting. They were overheard saying:

'It's the whole city of London.'
'It's the whole firework display.'
'It's the whole sky with all the stars.'

Figure 4.16 Engrossed in conversation together

Figure 4.17 Talking about their paintings

Figure 4.18 Sharing ideas together

'' Painting in the outdoor area did have a profound effect on the children's emotions. Their excitement, enjoyment and satisfaction led to increased confidence, which manifests itself in their energy, their constant interaction with each other and their use of language. ''

Sustained shared thinking

You might follow the children's interest in mini-beasts by trying to attract other creatures to the area. Buying or making bug boxes, a ladybird hotel and bird houses would be a good starting point, along with providing reference books and encouraging the children to examine the boxes and discuss what might come and live in them and where these boxes would be best placed (Figure 4.19).

Take time and care in your use of language to encourage a range of ideas, all of which should be accepted and valued, even if only some of them are feasible.

Through these experiences, children can:

Figure 4.19 Examining our bird and bee boxes

- Talk about what they are doing
- Think out loud
- Exchange ideas
- Listen to and discuss ideas
- Use different purposes for talk such as labelling, describing, predicting, explaining, hypothesising
- Using reference books in context
- Enjoy one another's company
- Begin to understand the rules of conversation.

Being active, less inhibited and free

Running

Children learn best through movement. They can be seen enjoying 'just running' in open spaces (Figures 4.20 and 4.21). This offers them the opportunity to be 'in tune' with their bodies as they experience being out of breath, their heart pounding and their limbs aching. You can use space within your nursery setting and also take children to the local parks so they can experience wide-open spaces.

Figure 4.20 Running with purpose

Figure 4.21 Developing a sense of freedom

Climbing, crawling and balancing

Settings that have large portable equipment, such as poles, planks, frames and ladders give children the opportunity to take calculated risks and gain greater control over their larger muscles. Children develop their muscle strength through climbing, crawling, moving themselves with their arms, pulling themselves through spaces and balancing. They need the opportunity to develop strength in their upper arms through hanging from bars and to feel what its like not to have their feet on the ground (Figure 4.22).

Figure 4.22 Hanging from a bar

Figures 4.23, 4.24 and 4.25 show a child finding out what her body can do as she climbs over one side of the A-frame to go down the other side, taking time to consider where to put her hands and feet.

Figure 4.23 So far so good!   Figure 4.24 This is the tricky bit!   Figure 4.25 I've managed on my own!

Other children spin their bodies around the parallel bars experiencing what it is like to hang upside down and move quickly.

If you don't have this equipment, you and the children can improvise by using planks, tyres and crates. In one nursery (Figure 4.26), a pile of logs provided children with the opportunity to clamber and balance as they climbed to the top.

Figure 4.26 Climbing carefully on logs

Bicycles

Before developing the outdoor space, many settings find that their most common piece of outdoor equipment is the three-wheeler bike. Limiting the space allocated to bicycles allows children to appreciate the other aspects of outdoor play. Actually, three-wheeler bikes do not offer challenge to most children. So where bikes are still used, make the environment more challenging by creating complex road ways and parking bays, and using road signs and road furniture. Restricting the use of three-wheeler bikes or providing children with two-wheeler bikes offers them a greater challenge and a sense of achievement (Figure 4.27).

Through these experiences, children can:

- Explore speed through running and riding bikes
- Control their bodies and stop
- Learn new skills
- Develop imaginative play
- Improvise, make decisions and solve problems
- Lift and carry
- Think about using equipment safely
- Work co-operatively
- Make links to real life, for example emergency vehicles.

Figure 4.27 Three-year-olds can ride two-wheeler bikes

Taking time out (reflecting)

Free-flow play allows children to set their own agendas and decide for themselves when they engage in quality play and when they need to rest or be alone to think. Access to indoors and outdoors throughout the day enables children to pace their own learning.

A tyre hanging from a tree offered the child in Figure 4.28 the opportunity to take 'time out' from the rest of the group. He spent some time sitting in the tyre after a long period of intense activity with a group of children at the blocks.

The group of girls in Figure 4.29 gathered some tyres together and used them as armchairs. They relaxed for a while together, comfortable in each other's company but not necessarily feeling the need to interact with one another.

Figure 4.28 Taking time to reflect and think

A child aged 5 years and 4 months who spent time in the quiet area outdoors said, 'It is just nice to sit and watch what the other children are doing.'

Through these experiences, children can:

- Be alone among others
- Watch the world go by
- Think their own thoughts
- Relax and 'just be'
- Recharge their batteries.

Figure 4.29 Relaxing together

The Elements

Snow

Exploit the elements and encourage the children to learn outside whatever the weather. Many of us are used to taking children out in snow (Figure 4.30), but some practitioners are less enthusiastic about taking children out in the rain and wind. The importance of seizing the opportunity to plan and enhance children's learning cannot be overestimated. Opportunities should be made for children to learn about the specific attributes of wind, rain, snow and ice.

During a cold spell, one nursery did not empty the water in the water tray (Figure 4.31). Instead, they took it outside and added a few resources. They placed an empty trough beside it for the children to make a comparison between frozen water and a sprinkling of snow.

Figure 4.30 Playing out in the snow

Figure 4.31 Using the elements to extend children's experiences

Similarly, children in a Reception class spent time trying to free the ice from their water trough and plant pots. They talked about the way water freezes, how heavy ice is and how sharp it can be when it cracks. The children left the ice on the grass commenting, 'in the sun it will melt.' The children compared the hardness of the ice with the softer ground and the crunchiness of the frozen grass in the shade.

Wind

In order for children to learn more about the effects of the elements, try hanging different types of material onto a tree over the space of a year. Encourage the children to observe and make comparisons about the changes that take place in these materials due to the elements.

On a windy day in March, the children, having noted the effect of the wind on the flimsy fabric, went inside and selected lengths of plastic ribbon from the creative area. They took these outside and were stimulated to dance by the effect of the wind on the streamers. Back in the classroom they told the other children that they had 'danced with the wind' (Figure 4.32). Later in the day, children found out that if they stood on the top of the climbing frame, the plastic ribbons flew higher than when they were on the ground.

Figure 4.32 Dancing in the wind

Rain

Being outside in the rain offers children a totally different experience to watching it from indoors, if they are given time to splash in puddles and touch the rain in order to feel what it is like. In Figure 4.33 we

Figure 4.33 Splashing in puddles

Figure 4.34 I can see circles

can see children exploring puddles and rain as it flowed from an umbrella. Children were also given time to observe the rain and one child commented, 'I can see circles' (Figure 4.34). Others watched coloured droplets disperse in water and made comments such as 'Look, a jelly fish' (Figure 4.35).

Figure 4.35 Can you see a jelly fish?

Sun

During the summer the children are able to access the outdoors more readily, and they have opportunities to explore the different effects of splashing in water without wellington boots. In Figure 4.36 we can see the joy children experience as they explore the coolness of water on their bare feet.

Warmer weather gives further opportunities for children to lounge in quiet areas 'reading' books, to make shadow drawings and to spend hours immersed in paddling pools or playing with hose pipes.

Through these experiences, children can:

- Engage in first-hand experiences
- Reflect on past experiences
- Make connections between experiences
- Explore and experiment
- Think about why things happen
- Talk about things of interest
- Understand the importance of water for plants and life.

Figure 4.36 Splashing with bare feet

Construction

Children can spend long periods of time building towers with large plastic bricks (Figure 4.37). A child chose to start building a tower on her own commenting, 'I building it up into the sky – and all on my own.' Later she decided that she needed help and asked another child, 'Come, get me some more yellow bricks.'

You might try providing a number of cardboard boxes for the children to pile high and work together to make really tall structures. Adults, chairs and steps are used as support when needed.

The children in Figure 4.38 had spent many days playing with cardboard boxes, creating enclosures and large buildings, but the fun did not stop there. The children's exploration and fun was heightened when one of the boxes they were using began to collapse. They continued their exploration of the box by experimenting to find out how many children it held.

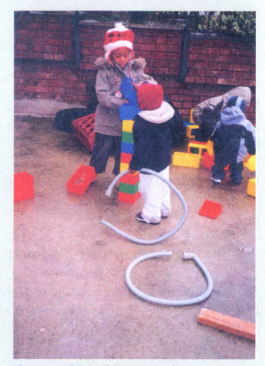

Figure 4.37 Building together

Opportunities for imaginative play are certainly enhanced when children are offered resources that enable them to build on a larger scale. Try acquiring bread and milk crates to give the children the opportunity to develop their own play scenarios and you're likely to see children talking at length, sharing ideas and negotiating during the building process (Figure 4.39). In Figure 4.40 we can see how the inclusion of a blanket with the bricks gives the children more options and opportunities for co-operative play.

Figure 4.38 Boxes are fun even when they collapse

Figure 4.39 Using crates to support imaginative play

Figure 4.40 Using blankets to change the space

Through these experiences, children can:

- Work alone or co-operatively with others
- Use language as a means of enlisting help, support or guidance
- Explore height and weight
- Develop imaginative play
- Use materials in a variety of ways.

Role play

Flexible resources enable children to develop their own interests and create their own role play scenarios with most of the activities organised and developed by the children themselves. These may range widely, from Power Ranger houses made from crates to hidey holes made by draping blankets over part of the climbing frame.

Taking children on visits focuses their attention and stimulates interest, as the following example shows.

A visit to a local garage was the stimulus for setting up a mechanic's workshop. Children devised their own rules for sharing bikes and ensuring they did not crash in to one another. They took on the roles of mechanics and police officers. They became familiar with the tools and took turns in fixing bikes.

Through these experiences, children can:

- Develop their own imaginative play situations
- Devise their own rules within the play situation
- Play together in changeable groups
- Consolidate newly acquired knowledge
- Use specific vocabulary in context
- Imitate adults in work situations and develop the role
- Widen their knowledge of the community in which they live.

Art ephemera

Art ephemera is an art form involving the collection and placement of materials found in the natural environment. The work of artists such as Andy Goldsworthy can act as an inspiration for the children. In Figures 4.41 and 4.42 we can see how a young child's interest in leaves developed into an art form. Whilst walking in the park he collected a few leaves. He observed them closely and then placed them on top of each other saying, 'I made a pile.' A digital camera was used to instantly record his work and the image used as a focus for later discussion.

Children can work together with sticks, stones, leaves, petals, seeds and flowers to form their own piece of art (Section 3C). The advantage of using these found materials is that they are abundant and replaceable. The art form can be made, recorded and changed as many times as the child wants.

Figure 4.41 Carefully examining a leaf

Figure 4.42 Piling leaves – an art form?

In Figure 4.43 two girls are working side by side, creating images on the ground. They have used the patterns created by the shadow of the fence as a guide for the border of the piece and placed the other objects in the centre.

Figure 4.43 Creating with found materials

Through these experiences, children can:

■ Observe found materials, closely focusing on patterns, shape and size
■ Consider how these materials look together
■ Create and re-create as often as they want
■ Work with natural materials within the environment
■ Be aware of the changes in natural found materials throughout the year.

Higher-order thinking

One of the most difficult aspects of early years work, but the most important, is to enable children to really think: to consider and think through their ideas.

Imaginative play

The children in Figure 4.44 were exploring making slopes with the long planks in the construction area. Another child joined in the play in his car and was asked, 'Can you drive it onto the ramp?' The two children engaged in a problem-solving discussion relating to the difficulties of driving the car onto the ramp. They were keen to look at how the car could be driven up the ramp with someone inside. This involved concentrating on the angle of the slope, which had to be much more gradual than the original construction. The children spent time going up and down the ramp as they worked out, through modifying the incline of the planks, how they could change the original construction to enable the car to stay on the ramp without toppling over. As it fell off on one attempt, they began to explore under the car and were interested in how they could mend it. This initiated another session of play about mechanics and included ways of 'jacking' up the car so that they could work on it.

Figure 4.44 The ramp

Construction

In one setting (Figure 4.45), the practitioner had brought in some planks from home to enable the children to do some work on designing and making. She talked with a small group and they decided how they wanted to use the planks and for what purpose. As it was the children's first experience of working with wood, they chose to use masking tape for joining. The practitioner supported this decision in order for the children to carry out their plans and see that their ideas could come to fruition. The children split into groups and began to talk about their intentions.

Figure 4.45 Making a house

One girl planned to make a house out of the wooden pieces. She carefully laid out the pieces to make the structure in a two-dimensional form. On completion, the child discussed the building with the practitioner and it became clear that, for the child, the most important part of the structure was the windows. These she had clearly defined by attaching masking tape to their perimeter.

In contrast, a small group of boys began to discuss what they would build and how. Their main priority was to be able to get inside the house that they had chosen to build (Figure 4.46).

Their conversations demonstrated that their thinking was concerned with ways that the house would be built so that it was upright and strong enough for them to get in and out. They chose to work in a small group and, after a lot of discussion and problem solving, incorporated a large cardboard box and a bread crate into the structure. They persisted in their task and built a three-dimensional shape that they were able to go inside. The boys talked together about how to position and fix the upright planks and how they could be connected to the crates in order to make the construction more stable.

Figure 4.46 Working together to build a house

Through these experiences children could:

- Explore ways of solving problems through trial and error, through testing and modifying their ideas
- Engage in imaginative play, making up their own scenarios
- Engage in listening to each other's ideas and testing them out
- Use mathematical language about slopes, length, height, width and speed
- Explore ways of joining materials together
- Gain a sense of achievement
- Choosing to work collaboratively or independently.

In this chapter we have considered how children enjoy learning outside. The cross-curricular nature of these experiences means that they can access all areas of the curriculum outdoors. We hope to have demonstrated the richness of the curriculum that can be accessed outdoors and to have raised questions about the amount of time children spend indoors!

5 Barriers and solutions

In this chapter we will be examining some issues to do with outdoor provision and play that are commonly perceived as 'problems'. These will be listed under the following categories:

- Vandalism
- Shared space
- Reluctance to change
- Management
- Storage
- Lack of direct access
- Restricted outdoor area
- Weather
- Foxes
- Financial consideration
- Parents and carers
- Risk management

Below are the suggestions of practical steps that have been seen to work for some settings. Because each location is different, you should try some and adapt others.

Vandalism

> We are based in an inner-city area and experience some vandalism, which is disheartening.

> This outdoor fun might be okay in a posh area but we come in the morning and there's condoms and syringes all over the place – a positive health hazard.

Solutions

- Organise resources on trolleys that are transportable. Take them in at night.
- Research shows that an area that appears unkempt is more likely to be vandalised, so try to keep outside areas well maintained.
- Buy easily replaceable resources, e.g. saucepans and spoons from car boot sales for your music area and CDs to hang on trees.
- Include young people in the community in the design and upkeep of your outdoor area so that they feel some ownership of it.
- Encouraging a sense of ownership has been found to develop care for the environment and reduce damage and vandalism. Installing defensive measures may have an unintended effect of restricting people with mobility impairments.
- Ask local police to patrol the area during the evening.
- Check the area each morning to ensure its safety.
- Put up letters in the garden from the children asking people to take care of it.

Shared space

Many settings do not have an allocated outdoor space.

> ' We are based in a church and our only play space is in the car park – not ideal! We don't want to lose any of our charges but also we don't want to deprive them of outdoor experiences. Any ideas? '

Solutions

■ Buy or have made temporary, moveable fences to section off part of the car park.
■ Go and find out about local facilities and take children out regularly (Figure 5.1).
■ Talk to the parish council about any proposed changes.
■ Think about using the features you have to the best advantage.

Figure 5.1 Extending children's experiences through local visits

> ' In our primary school, the Nursery and Reception class use the outside area at lunchtime under the supervision of a midday supervisor. The children's behaviour deteriorates during this time and they wreck the place. What can we do? '

Solutions

■ Develop consistent expectations of children's behaviour.
■ Consider asking the early years team to work a shift system to cover the lunch period.
■ Ensure that the environment is suitably stimulating for the older children.
■ Consider a whole-school approach in order to ensure that Reception classes have direct access to the outdoor environment.

■ Organise whole-staff training, including midday supervisors.

Reluctance to change

> *We find it easier to organise our day by having all the children in or out. It means we know where all the children are and we are sure that we maintain our ratios. We know we need to change but how?*

Solutions

■ Organise whole-team training to enable staff to see the indoor and outdoor areas as two halves of a whole learning environment and not just a place to let off steam.
■ Review interview questions so that you employ practitioners who value outdoor play.
■ Include working with children outdoors as part of staff appraisal.
■ Ensure that everyone knows that outdoor play is a legal entitlement as stated in the Day Care Standards (Ofsted 2001) and the Curriculum Guidance for the Foundation Stage (QCA 2000).
■ When children are engaged in free-flow play indoors and outdoors, they are more likely to play for longer periods of time and concentrate at a deeper level. This makes working with the children easier and more fun.
■ Ensure that staff understand that the routine is for the children and not for the adults.

Management

> *I am a newly qualified teacher in a Reception class. I know my children should have free-flow access to outside but my head teacher says they must stick to a 15-minute playtime. I don't want to fail my induction year. Help!*

Solutions

■ Bring in recent literature on outdoor play to show head teacher/manager.
■ Speak to your Mentor, Foundation Stage Co-ordinator or Early Years Advisory Teacher to gain support for your view.
■ Find out where there are examples of good practice and ask your head teacher/manager to visit with you.
■ Discover what the head teacher/manager's concerns are regarding extending outdoor play and hold a staff meeting to share ideas.

Storage

Many people identified the problems associated with storage – inadequate size, possibility of vandalism, full of spiders, damp, no outside storage.

> *Our little cupboard is too small, toys are piled on top of each other, so the same things come out every day.*

> *We never dared get a shed in case it got burnt down at the weekend.*

Solutions

- Have storage where you can reach everything.
- Store weather boxes indoors to be brought out when appropriate.
- Buy sheds from local DIY stores: there are lots of different types now.
- Use trolleys to store equipment and wheel them out at the beginning of the day.
- Buy a metal shed if fire damage is a risk.
- Give children the responsibility for taking out resources if they have to be stored inside.
- Ask other users of the premises, for example scout leaders, if you could share their storage facilities.
- Keep equipment in bags that can be stored on the fence.

> **We love our outdoor area and as a staff team we're really good at accessing cheap resources from car-boot sales. Some of the things can be left out but we would really welcome advice about storage. Which works best? Any ideas?**

Solutions

- Use low-level shelving that children can access either via a door or a screen that rolls/lifts up.
- Clear away duplicates or unwanted equipment to create space for the essentials.
- Label all resources clearly and make a plan of where things are stored.
- Use transparent boxes for portable equipment.
- Invest in a canopy with a windshield or a caravan awning around the sheltered area.
- Use a mini greenhouse.
- Put carrier bags with sorted equipment on walls and fences.
- Use shoe pockets for small items, e.g. lenses, magnets.

Lack of direct access

Many settings have problems with unsupervised spaces, especially when children have to walk along corridors to get to the outdoor area.

> **The children have to walk past the toilets to get to the outside area. They may go in there to play if they are unsupervised.**

Solutions

- Teach the children how to behave in different situations.
- Allocate one practitioner as a 'float' to support children going outdoors.
- Put up notices to remind children about the route to outdoors and the expectations.
- Reassure practitioners that children will behave responsibly. Ask them to observe and monitor children.
- Ensure children go out in pairs, and allocate a more experienced child to accompany a younger one.
- Set up a signing-in and signing-out board with Velcro names/pictures so you know which children are outdoors.

Restricted outdoor area

> **Our outdoor area is very small. It is difficult for us to implement all these ideas about outdoor play that we hear about. Is there anything we can do?**

Solutions

- Arrange visits in the local area (e.g. market, walks to the post box) through the week.
- Use the local park for large movement and set up smaller scale activities in the garden, for example bird feeders, window boxes.
- Bring outdoor play inside and let the children explore crates and tubing, etc. (Figure 5.2).
- Negotiate with others to increase the size of the area.
- Consider moving premises!

Figure 5.2 Making use of crates and tyres indoors

> **Children are not allowed on the grass. They are only allowed on the safety surface area.**

Solutions

- Ask for wellington boots and teach the children to put them on independently.
- Talk to children about the expectations of how to play safely outdoors.
- Hold a parents' meeting to share the importance of 'managed risk'.

Children will stay outdoors all the time

> **We are worried that our children will spend all their time outdoors if the door is open all the time.**

Solutions

- This will be an issue at the beginning, until children are reassured that the outdoor will not be withdrawn again.
- Consider the provision as a whole and over a period of time.
- Extend the time on offer outdoors and offer children the choice. It may take several weeks before children realise that they can play in both areas.
- Plan focused activities for target children indoors and outdoors.
- Support and extend children's play, for example if they need masks for outdoor role play, help them to make these indoors.
- Provide interesting activities indoors on different levels, for example on the floor and standing as well as table-top activities.

Bad weather

> I find it so difficult to get excited about outdoor play. It's always raining in England and even on dry days the kids come in with mud all over their shoes and our lovely wooden floor looks AWFUL.

Solutions

- Buy umbrellas and wellington boots and splash suits for younger children.
- Make a list of activities suitable for rainy days (Section 3G).
- Stock a rainy day weather box (Section 3E).
- Wait for the heaviest rain to pass – it rarely rains all day long – and be ready for the break (there may even be a rainbow).
- Remember that children do not notice that it's cold and wet so much as long as they are dry and warm soon after.
- Put down a protective floor covering on both sides of the adjoining door and provide seating for changing and storing shoes.
- Lay an old piece of carpet over a muddy patch so children can move in and out freely.
- In Finland they only stop taking children out when it gets to minus 15 °C.

Foxes

> We planted a lovely flower garden but the foxes dug up the bulbs and poohed in the bed. Yuk! We don't want to go out any more – it's too disheartening.

Solutions

- Complaints against urban foxes are rare and usually trivial or without foundation.
- Whilst foxes will kill small pets such as guinea pigs, this risk will be minimised by building secure hutches and practising diligent husbandry.
- Foxes are very unlikely to spread disease to humans or their pets.
- To repel foxes, use a suitable proprietary animal repellent (creosote is banned).
- Get a sound-alert box.

Parents

> It's all right for you to say children should be outside, but our parents and grandparents won't let them because they are concerned about their health. They don't want them getting pneumonia or falling over – let alone eating worms.

> We work in partnership with parents, so only go out on the warmest days now.

Solutions

- Talk to parents about the importance of outdoor play and the children's entitlement to outdoor play.
- Ask parents to give practical support in developing the outdoor area.
- Send out articles and alert parents to the health risks associated with lack of exercise.
- Send out newsletters updating parents with progress.
- Hold a workshop regarding outdoor play led by the early years team and/or the Early Years Advisory Teacher.
- Display photographs of children learning outdoors.
- Invite parents to come and watch their children playing outdoors.
- Ask parents what and where they remember playing as a child.

Financial considerations

> We don't have much money to spend on our outdoor area. How can we provide interesting things for the children to do?

Solutions

- Apply for a grant from a recognised charity.
- Ask local shops/stores if you can be added to their list of contacts to receive excess/surplus goods.
- Find cheap or free resources (Section 3B).
- Discover your local recycling centre or scrap bank.
- Collect resources to build up resource boxes from your existing materials (Section 3E).
- Ask parents to donate items, for example heavy curtains and unwanted wallpaper, guttering or pipes.
- Make collections of resources with the children, for example plastic bottles for skittles.

Risk management

> We are concerned about the risk to children during outdoor play and how we can allay parents' fears.

- Practitioners recognised that their role requires a balance of protection that also enables challenge.
- Adults may want to ban activities they do not value and which make them anxious. However, the memories that adults value are all about activity, risk, challenge and excitement.
- Without challenges and risks, children will find play areas uninteresting or use them in inappropriate ways, which become dangerous.

■ Children with additional needs are more likely to be overprotected and have restricted experiences, although these approaches are not usually based on reasonable risk assessment.

■ There is a feeling that too much emphasis is being placed on children's safety and that this is stifling the freedom and development of the children it is meant to protect.

■ The Child Accident Prevention Trust recognises that experimentation and risk-taking are part of growing up.

■ Risk assessment can strike a balance between the benefits and risks of play, taking into account the age and abilities of the children.

■ DEMOS research (Thomas and Thompson 2004) found that assessing danger is children's top priority when thinking about different environments.

■ Lady Allen of Hurtwood (in John and Wheway 2004) noted that children with additional needs can lead an unnecessarily limited life. They are often overprotected and are rarely allowed to take risks. Titman (1994) states, 'If any child is prevented from playing then it diminishes the play experience for all.'

■ Because of restrictions in an increasingly dangerous world, nursery and school grounds become symbolic of a safe haven and ever more important.

■ A 'can do' approach allows for problems to be overcome with goodwill rather than play being prevented until remedial action is undertaken.

■ Remember that children with additional needs may find outdoor breaks the most traumatic times of the day, associated with bullying and feeling left out.

We should

■ Problem solve with children to help them recognise risk level and deal with dangers.

■ Show children sensible practice in handling common accidents.

■ Understand parents' concerns and make them part of the problem solving.

■ Consider the danger to the health and well-being of children if there is an overcautious application of recommendations and guidance.

■ Refer to 'Managing risk in play provision' Play Safety Forum statement (www.ncb.org.uk).

■ All children need and want to take risks in order to explore limits, venture into new experiences and develop their capabilities from a very young age and from their earliest play experiences. Children would never learn to walk, climb stairs or ride a bicycle unless they were strongly motivated to respond to challenges involving a risk of injury. Children with disabilities have an equal, if not greater need for opportunities to take risks, since they may be denied the freedom of choice enjoyed by their non-disabled peers.

Conclusion

It is inspiring to see how practitioners overcome obstacles to outdoor play, whether the difficulties are large or small. As confidence and belief in the necessity for outdoor play grows, they adopt a practical response to barriers and find a range of solutions. Imaginative and resourceful thinking is essential when overcoming barriers to outdoor play. Some issues are hard to resolve but team efforts often prove effective in bringing about solutions or compromises to barriers which appeared insurmountable at the outset.

6 Benefits of outdoor play

In this chapter we summarise some of the benefits of outdoor play for children, practitioners and parents. As the findings may have been mentioned in previous chapters, we intend only to summarise them here.

The benefits of outdoor play for the children involved in the Brent project

For the purpose of this chapter we will divide the ways that children benefited from the project into three categories:

- Benefits to children's health
- Ways in which children's attitude toward the outdoors changed
- Things children learnt.

Benefits to children's health

- Instances of ill health lessened. Several project leaders reviewed the attendance records and noted that the instances of illness were less than they had been during the previous year. This they attributed to children accessing outdoors more often, thus preventing the spread of infection when children spend long periods of time in warm, stuffy rooms.
- Children have become more robust as they have experienced longer periods of play outdoors or have been taken out daily. Access to the outdoor environment on a daily basis ensures that children experience all weathers and learn how to protect themselves with appropriate footwear, clothing or creams.
- Children have more opportunity for play, which develops their large muscle groups and heart and lung functions, thus making them healthier.
- Children were reported to judge risk more accurately and fewer accidents were recorded within the settings when both indoors and outdoors were made available at the same time. Project leaders thought this was due to the fact that children were confident that they would be going out every day and were therefore less 'frenetic' when the doors were opened.

A change of attitude for the children

Practitioners noted many changes in the children's behaviour and attitudes to learning. The most significant of which was the increased motivation that many showed. Additional benefits are described below.

- Children became more independent when given the choice to be indoors or outdoors and took responsibility for putting on their own outdoor clothing and wellington boots.

- Some children were observed concentrating for long periods of time outdoors, and practitioners assumed that this was because they were engrossed in their play and had made their own choices as to whether to play indoors or stay outdoors.
- High levels of involvement were observed as children were engaged in deep-level learning.
- Many children developed an 'I can' approach to learning, based on the new-found confidence in their own abilities within the outdoor environment. Their increasing competence generated confidence and self-esteem, a sense of mastery and well-being.
- Children took on more responsibilities, such as deciding which resources to use, selecting them from accessible units and returning them independently. They also became more responsible for the environment and noticed, for example, when the bird feeder was empty.
- Examples of challenging behaviour were less frequent and children's ability to resolve their own conflicts grew.
- Children were also making links between their outdoor play and their life experiences. They were taking control of their own learning and returning the following day with materials from home to enhance their play.

What the children learnt

The opportunities for children's learning during the project were immense, and some of the experiences encountered were only possible outdoors. We have listed some of them below.

- Children became more physically able and aware of what their bodies could do. They were helped to reflect upon their achievements and be respectful of the abilities of others.
- Freedom of movement gave children the opportunity to learn about their position in space. They were also able to engage in first-hand experiences of speed, swirling, height, weight and growth.
- Many children who never picked a book up inside were observed sitting 'reading' outside.
- When real situations with real problems were presented outdoors, children were observed to be more expressive, asking questions and discussing ideas together.
- Boys appeared more confident to engage in literacy activities outdoors. They experienced different purposes for writing such as list-making, writing invitations and messages, completing forms and leaving messages.
- Boys also appeared to be more involved in imaginative play, such as the mechanics workshop or the pizza delivery service. These imaginative scenarios engaged children in purposeful, contextualised cross-curricular experiences.
- Children with English as an additional language seemed to become more confident communicators. They were observed talking in the calmer areas of the outdoors, in places that were less obviously observed by an adult.
- Children who were given the opportunity to work with children older and younger than themselves appeared to play well together. When this was in a school situation, the transition between Nursery and Reception was made easier.
- Flexible, open-ended materials gave children an opportunity to learn more about the process of negotiation and decision-making, as they created play scenarios for themselves. Once they had organised the materials they either played co-operatively together or were able to relax and to sit back and watch what other children did.
- Through active exploration, the children accessed a broad curriculum, and, as many practitioners stated, 'the opportunities are endless'.

- Children developed a sense of awe and wonder at the beauty of the natural environment. They spent time noticing the formation of snowflakes and the structure of spider webs, and regularly took in objects from outside to look at under the microscope on the computer.
- Given time, the children developed a respect for living creatures and moved from a 'stamp on it' mentality to a 'let's make a home for it' attitude.
- The fear of living creatures reduced as the children had the opportunity to see mini-beasts in their natural environment. Children observed from a distance, identifying the mini-beasts in books or on the computer. Gradually, as their confidence grew, they took a closer look at the characteristics of the live creatures.

Practitioners

- They were more confident in their role outdoors and its implications.
- They were more aware of the potential learning opportunities within the outdoor environment.
- They appreciated the value of open-ended resources and organised others to collect appropriate resources.
- They observed children more closely, 'tuning into the children' and anticipating their needs and planning appropriately.

Many practitioners actively listened to the children in their setting, and together they began to plan developments within the outdoor environment. This enabled a mutual trust to develop between the children and the practitioners – a trust that they would use the outdoor environment every day and take full advantage of the various opportunities that the weather in this country provides.

- Practitioners took full advantage of the opportunity to observe all aspects of the children's behaviour and gradually began to trust the children to use the resources independently and judge what they can and cannot do for themselves.
- Practitioners observed and trusted children to calculate risks for themselves and act accordingly.
- Practitioners 'fine tuned' their ability to observe, listen and judge whether it was appropriate to step in and intervene or support a child.

This slight change in the behaviour of the practitioners resulted in significant changes in the behaviour of the children.

- Practitioners recorded a reduced number of conflicts when both indoor and outdoor play was on offer for long lengths of time on a daily basis. They noticed a calmer atmosphere within the settings as the children had more opportunities and experiences on offer to them, which in turn reduced the element of competition and gave the children time to choose and follow the flow of their play.
- Practitioners noted improved behaviour in the children when they were outdoors. They appeared to be more purposeful in their play and less anxious to 'get out there first to grab the bike'.
- Practitioners noticed that some children were much more confident outdoors, and this had a direct impact on all areas of their development. As the children spent more time outdoors doing things they could do, their play became more complex and they began to incorporate aspects of literacy and numeracy into it. This empowered them to become more able learners inside.

Parents

Initially there were mixed reactions from the parents, but practitioners commented on the value of keeping parents informed.

- Involving parents from the beginning increased their understanding, interest and support. It gave them the opportunity to ask questions and make contributions. It also enabled parents to feel a part of the setting and more a part of the child's life at nursery.
- Some parents relished the chance to be actively involved in the setting and share their passion for the outdoors. Others made contributions of shrubs and plants, or organised fund-raising activities.
- Gradually, parents began to appreciate the learning that could take place outdoors and were pleased that children came home 'refreshed not frustrated'.
- Parents appreciated the need to send children suitably clothed and often provided wellington boots for the children to use while at nursery/school.
- Over time the parents were reassured of the benefits of outdoor play for their children's health. Many commented on improvements to their child's eating habits, sleep patterns, complexion and general health.

Conclusion

We found that the outdoor project refreshed the minds of both the children and the practitioners, and enabled the parents to become involved in the life of their children's nursery or school.

FORMS AND CHECKLISTS

On the Internet

On the publisher's website http://www.routledgeteachers.com you will find the following adaptable and photocopiable pro formas for developing and monitoring outdoor provision:

- Action plan for outdoor area
- Timeline for developing outdoor provision
- General action plan
- Mini action plans for outdoor learning bays
- Individual Educator Audit
- Monitoring sheet for use of areas.

In the book

In the rest of this section you will find:

- An observation checklist
- A self-evaluation of outdoor play.

Observation checklist

The following questions are set out for project leaders to review their provision through observations. The answers could form the basis for staff meetings on the effectiveness of the provision.

- Does the outdoor area create opportunities for the children to speak, listen and represent ideas?
- What languages do the children use outdoors?
- Are the children developing mathematical skills, for example using the hopscotch to count in sequence, comparing logs and describing the properties of shapes?
- Are the children building friendships, interacting, having opportunities for problem solving, which help them to gain confidence?
- Are the children looking after the environment?
- How are the children developing gross and fine motor movements?
- Are the children given plenty of time to explore, to experiment and to refine movements and actions?
- Do the children learn through their senses, for example by looking at things from different perspectives? Smelling flowers after the rain?
- What type of creative things do the children do outdoors?
- Do the children use their imaginations, respond, explore, express and communicate their ideas?
- Are the children taking risks and learning from their mistakes?
- What type of experiences do the children have outdoors, for example hands-on experiences, contact with nature?

Self-evaluation of outdoor play

Managers, head teachers, co-ordinators, or Early Years Advisory Teachers who wish to evaluate a setting's outdoor provision may find this checklist useful. Reflecting on the key issues identified may help in promoting high quality outdoor provision. You may wish to tick the relevant boxes and add comments.

Evaluating the outdoor play area

- [ ] Is the outdoor learning environment stimulating/challenging?
- [ ] Do the outdoor experiences meet the needs of all the children?
- [ ] Do practitioners capitalise on the learning opportunities outdoors?
- [ ] Are parents involved in outdoor play?
- [ ] Do children, practitioners and parents enjoy and value outdoor learning?
- [ ] Is there a policy for outdoor play?
- [ ] Do the team undertake outdoor play training?

Management of outdoor area

- [ ] Is there a clear management structure for outdoor play?
- [ ] Does the manager/head teacher value, support and fund outdoor play effectively?
- [ ] Does the setting improvement plan include areas for development outdoors?
- [ ] Is there a named practitioner responsible for the upkeep of a particular bay/trolley?
- [ ] Are practitioners deployed between indoor and outdoor play areas effectively?
- [ ] Is there a procedure to check the equipment and area for safety?
- [ ] Is the area monitored regularly to see how practitioners and the children use it?
- [ ] Is outdoor play evaluated appropriately?

Outdoor learning environment

Consider the following features in terms of their suitability for the particular area:

Design

- [ ] Access – Are there suitable pathways and fences?
- [ ] Size – Are there spaces to run in, hide in, etc.?
- [ ] Layout – Is the outdoor area organised into resource-based learning bays?

☐ Fixed equipment – Does this enhance the provision?

☐ Surfaces – Is there a variety of surfaces for children to play on?

☐ Seating – Does seating enhance learning opportunities?

☐ Storage – Is it suitable for the equipment and easily accessible for practitioners and children?

☐ Weather – Do practitioners capitalise on different weather conditions?

☐ Safety – Is a safe yet challenging environment maintained?

☐ Look of the area – Are there a range of appealing, natural features?

Resourcing

☐ Are there lists of equipment for each bay/trolley, so a wide range of resources is available all day every day?

☐ Are all the outdoor bays imaginatively laid out and well resourced?

☐ Are each of the bays equally inviting to children from a range of cultures, boys and girls, children with additional needs?

☐ Are the equipment and materials well presented?

☐ Is there a range of appropriate equipment and does it offer challenge?

☐ Is the equipment of good quality – does it extend children's imagination, experiences and emotions?

☐ Does the equipment promote non-stereotypical play?

☐ Does the equipment promote girls and boys equal access to the area (i.e. non-gender specific)?

☐ Have the needs of children with disabilities been considered, e.g. benches with backs, bright or contrasting colours identifying sudden or unexpected changes in level, path, edges, etc?

☐ Do the resources relate to the children's own experiences?

☐ Do the resources encourage children to develop positive attitudes and dispositions?

Practitioners outdoors

☐ Are observations carried out to see how children use the resources?

☐ Are observations used to inform planning?

☐ Do practitioners interact with children, extend their interests and develop their understanding?

☐ Are practitioners able to sustain and develop play outdoors?

☐ Are specific skills taught appropriately and confidently?

☐ Do practitioners provide positive role models?

☐ Do practitioners use appropriate language?

☐ Are practitioners knowledgeable about learning that can/does take place outdoors?

☐ Are all practitioners involved in planning for outdoors?

☐ Is other documentation used, for example photographs, samples of work and video clips to add to the portfolio and share with parents?

☐ Is an atmosphere created where each child feels secure?

Children outdoors

☐ Are children offered long periods of uninterrupted outdoor play?

☐ Can children choose when they want to go out?

☐ Are children eager and enthusiastic about their outdoor learning?

☐ Do they have access to free-flow play between outdoors and indoors?

☐ Can all children access outdoor play?

☐ Can children make decisions about how and where they use the equipment?

☐ Do both boys and girls use the equipment?

☐ Does each child participate in a range of activities?

☐ Are there opportunities to work on a large scale?

☐ Do children exercise their bodies to raise their heart rate?

☐ Do they play co-operatively?

☐ Do children experience a broad and balanced curriculum outdoors?

☐ Are children encouraged to take a role in caring for the outdoor environment?

Parents

☐ Are parents kept informed about the learning that takes place outdoors and included in planning?

☐ Does the setting share its intentions for outdoor learning with parents?

☐ Is each child's learning outdoors shared with her/his parents?

☐ Are parents included in future developments for the outdoor area?

Further comments or reflection

SECTION 3

FURTHER IDEAS AND MATERIALS TO DEVELOP OUTDOOR PROVISION

Contents

3A Starting to develop the outdoor area

3B Using found and recycled materials

3C Using natural materials

3D ICT and the outdoor curriculum

3E Resource boxes

3F Developing the potential of walls and corners

3G Ideas for outdoor play during autumn, winter and early spring

3A Starting to develop the outdoor area

Here are some ways in which you might develop your outdoor project:

- Write an action plan supported by manager/head teacher.
- Keep photographs of before and after.
- Collect views of all staff.
- Ask parents and local companies for free resources.
- Ask children for their responses to outdoor play.
- Make a plan of the outdoor area.
- Collect observations of outdoor play.
- Develop an outdoor policy (which might be part of a Foundation Stage policy).

3B Using found and recycled materials

(With thanks to Lucky Khera, Strathmore Infants)

Resource	Activity
Tyres	Physical skills, e.g. rolling, building, balancing
	Obstacle course, use tyres to balance a plank
	Place tyres on top of each other at varying heights and use as targets for children to throw balls into and score how many balls they get in
	Use tyres with guttering to create a ball run
	Create shape- and pattern-making tyre prints
	Use in imaginative role-play with crates and boxes to make fire engine, cars, etc.
Cardboard boxes	Inspire children's construction skills, e.g. a huge cardboard box becomes a castle, house or space rocket to be decorated by children
	Make dens, tunnels or hidden areas
Pipes	Use for construction
	Use to test water flow to enhance problem solving
	Introduce predicting and making decisions (If there is a leak, what is causing it? Why does the water take a long time to travel through the pipe?)
Guttering	Experiment to see how water travels, observing different water levels in the guttering
	Roll balls from varying heights and along different slopes
	Make bridges for cars to travel along and investigate problems (How can you make the cars travel faster/slower? Do you think the balls will travel faster than the cars? How can we find out?)
Crates	Imaginative role play, e.g. making police cars, delivery trucks
	Use guttering to roll a variety of balls into crates, and children count how many they got in
	Store bottles for water play and children sort bottles into different crates

Resource	Activity
Buckets	Children can freely throw balls or beanbags at buckets and count how many beanbags they get in the buckets and how many land on the ground, saying whether more landed on the ground or in the bucket
	Number buckets for children to throw balls and beanbags into; write their scores
	Make pulleys using buckets and ropes, and fill the buckets with water, leaves, twigs, etc.
Fabric	Children can initiate their own ideas such as tents, rivers, magic tunnels, caves, pathways, etc.
Chalk	Make marks, patterns, shapes, pictures on the ground or walls
	Make shapes on the walls and throw balls/beanbags at the shapes as described (Can you aim at the one with the curved edge? Which shape are you aiming at? Can you hit the square first and the circle second? Which shape did you hit with the second/third beanbag?)
	Chalk a numbered track on the floor for a variety of number games, or chalk wavy lines to walk on
Tins	Make music by hanging various-sized tins for the children to bang, leave a selection on the ground
	Count how many different types of objects you can place into each tin
	Why do some tins hold more/less, are heavy/light, are big/small?
	Order tins according to size, volume, capacity, using different-sized bottles to fill the tins
Wood	Use wooden blocks collected from a timber merchant for construction
	Hammer nails, make models
	Place large blocks onto the ground as a balancing beam
Bottles and balls	Hang up bottles with small amounts of coloured water and then throw balls at the bottles to improve physical skills
	Use bottles as skittles, some empty, some with water/sand (How many did you knock down? You hit two more on your second throw, now how many have you knocked down? Can we write down how many you knocked down altogether? How can we see who knocked down the most at the end of the game?)
	Use balls as skittles, by throwing beanbags at balls, or use bats to hit balls

Resource	Activity
Paintbrushes and water	Use coloured or plain water to make marks, paint patterns, their names, shapes, etc. and experiment freely, observing and learning as it evaporates away in the sunshine
	How can you record the shapes you painted with water so that you can remember what you did?
	Paint the fence/outdoor shed being 'builders and decorators'
Rope	Place rope on the ground and walk on to practise balancing skills
	Hang rope from trees to climb, swing, pull, etc.
	Use rope when making large constructions using crates, boxes
	Make shapes on the ground with rope. (Can you describe the shape you have made? Can you give your shape a name? Can you record the shape you have made?)
Logs	Balance on!
	Use chopped-up logs to jump on/off
	Use as stepping stones, to sit and read, socialise with peers/adults
Bicycle wheels	Use as a water wheel
	Use for weaving
	Use as part of imaginative role-play, e.g. the wheel to a fire engine, a pirate-ship wheel
CDs	Hang CDs outdoors – great reflections in the sun
	Use soft balls to aim at CDs and make a tally chart of scores
Carpet squares	Ideal for outdoor snack-time
	Lay carpet squares down and use them as paving stones, moving in the different directions – forward, sideways or backwards
	Play 'Musical squares': Skip, jog, jump around the area, but when a colour is called sit on a carpet square of that colour
Telephones and clipboards	Create a conversation table by placing telephones, paper and pens – to promote speaking, listening, mark-making and number skills
	Drawing on a clipboard what you find in the garden
	Use clipboards as part of outdoor role-play set-ups, e.g. cafe, parking tickets, number, letter, shape hunt, detective work, etc.

3C Using natural materials

Material	Activity
Leaves	Create patterns with leaves
	Arrange leaves according to size, shape, colour, favourites
	Look at symmetry of leaves with mirrors
	Use laminated leaves to match with leaves found outside
	Throw leaves up in the air
	Fill builders' trays with leaves, conkers, other seeds, compost (and toy mini-beasts)
	Thread autumn leaves and hang from canopy or tree to catch light
	Make leaf prints in large slabs of clay
	Find leaf skeletons and examine them with hand lens and torch, shining light onto paper
	Smell the scent of evergreens
Twigs, bark	Make a wool-weaving on a tree or branch
	Lift up pieces of wood to find mini-beasts
	Use branches for printing
	Create a huge outline, e.g. dinosaur skeletons
	Build bonfires
	Make tents and tepees with long sticks and drapes
	Tie twigs together with bark strips
	Make bark rubbings
	Explore bark chipping in a paddling pool or builders' tray
	Use bark chippings in small world play
	Whittle and peel off bark, particularly silver birch
	Use a measuring stick to find out how tall are you
	Play 'Pooh sticks' in guttering and moving water
	Weave bendy twigs like willow and evergreens into fencing

Pebbles	Transport stones and pebbles in a wheelbarrow
	Make stone sculptures
	Build a cairn by adding stones to a heap
	Clean and polish pebbles or paint and varnish stones
	Add pebbles to sand and water
	Explore stones or coloured gravel in tyres
	Make patterns using stones, including rangoli (an Indian art form using symmetrical patters)
	Make textured paths with varied rocks, shingle, slate
	Make an archaeological dig and brush away sand, stones
	Set stones in clay to create tiles
	Provide different-sized containers, how many stones can you fit into each container? Which container has more/less? How many stones do we need to put into this container so that both containers have the same amount?
Seeds	Make potions by mixing seeds, petals, etc. with water
	Compare seeds before planting, e.g. large bean seeds and tiny lettuce seeds
	Throw sycamore seeds, lime seeds into the air
	Collect conkers, beech nuts, acorns, etc. and use to make people or pictures, attaching with pins or Blu-Tack
	Plant seeds in tubs and track growth
Grass, flowers, twigs, leaves, blades of grass	Can you sort what you have found? Can you sort the items and make a collage to record what you have found?
	Make a large flower design using the natural items that children have found (using a hoop for the head of the flower)
	Children can make soup using twigs, soil, leaves, etc.
General	Attach pieces of natural materials to a masking-tape bracelet as a map of where you've been on a walk or garden trail
	Place hanging baskets full of natural materials at low level
	Plant tubs of scented herbs, e.g. lavender and link to rhymes
	Make smelly socks filled with herbs, orange peel, pine cones that can be batted
	Make wind chimes with shells and sticks
	Fill pots with large seeds and use as shakers to accompany dancing

3D ICT and the outdoor curriculum

In the Curriculum Guidance (QCA 2000) the wider use of ICT in the environment is recognised and the document recommends that all settings should encourage this. The following suggestions relate to how ICT can be used in the outdoor curriculum as a tool to support children's learning rather than as an end in itself. ICT is 'More than Computers' (Siraj-Blatchford 2003) and there are many ways to support a collaborative approach to using ICT in meaningful situations outdoors.

Children are born into a technological age and are fascinated by what happens at the touch of a button. 'Talking with children as they explore technologies will help them to see why things happen and how things work' (Kennington 2005: 2).

In the outdoor environment there are many real and role-play examples of how ICT can be effectively integrated into the provision. In the following chart, the resources are categorised as things from everyday life, audio and standalone devices.

Hardware/suggestion	Ideas for using ICT in the outdoor curriculum
Audio: Speaking and listening	
Mobile phones	Children are often very familiar with mobile phones. Use in various role-play situations (garden shop enquiries, ordering food, emergency vehicles, etc.).
	Offer children an opportunity to phone their families, occasionally to have a conversation about what they are doing in the setting. Also text relatives and friends in role-play situations.
Headset walkie-talkies	Police, ambulance, traffic wardens, pilots and estate agents all find walkie-talkies useful. Taxi booking firms also use headsets. These resources offer children plenty of opportunities to visit different locations by taxi (and bikes).
MP3 players	Useful for playing music for dancing to outdoors. Also for story telling, particularly to recreate a story such as *Rosie's Walk* (P. Hutchins, 2001, Red Fox, ISBN 009941399) or *We're Going on a Bear Hunt* (M. Rosen and H. Oxenbury, 1993, Walker Books, ISBN 0744523230). Features from the story can be recreated outdoors, e.g. cave.
Battery-operated cassette recorder	Tape sounds outdoors – bird song, traffic. Children can create their own listening games. Also useful for recording stories which children invent outdoors. Add short tapes to story sacks.

Radio mike	With a stage made from pallets or boxes the next Pop Idol can appear.
	Children can sing, perform or even present the news or a wildlife show holding a radio mike.
Karaoke	These are great fun especially with a stage. You will need a convenient window so that the machine can be plugged in indoors. The freedom of space and the opportunity to make more noise outdoors are very suitable for karaoke.
Standalone devices	
Digital cameras	For use by both adults and children after suitable introduction and safety talk.
	Children can photograph aspects of the outdoor area that they particularly enjoy or do not like. If laminated, these can be displayed outdoors with children's comments for parents and visitors to read.
	Use the zoom to take close up pictures of mini-beasts, frozen leaves and other outdoor finds. Make a slide show of the images on the computer indoors to give an enlarged version.
	Use as a stimulus for art by taking pictures, e.g. flowers, lorries, marbling in puddles, snowy days.
	Invaluable for recording significant moments in children's learning and adding to portfolios to share with parents.
CCTV	Buy an inexpensive one from DIY store (check if it is suitable for outdoor use) and ask for old black and white monitors. Set up in two different parts of the nursery so children can watch their friends.
Video recorder	Video children's play in the outdoor area. Give the children the videotape to play later indoors.
	Very helpful for asking children to reflect on their own learning in active play, e.g. climbing, playing 'What's the time Mr Wolf?', when it is difficult to record children's responses.
Intel Digital Blue Movie Camera	Small and easy to hold. Ideal for children to use to take short video clips outdoors or still images. Can be used to retell sequences of play and for children to write their own scripts to accompany the video.
Metal detector – child-size	Use in sand or digging area with planted treasure. Add magnets to the sand/digging area.
Hand-held metal detector	Put metal objects such as ball bearings into flowerpots, under bushes and ask children if they can find them all. Support children in this by having numbered cards. Link to pirate themes, car mechanics, etc.

Remote-control cars, programmable toys, e.g. Pixie (see below)	Set up a course and ask children to estimate the distances. Construct a rally team and let children share ideas and fine tune their steering techniques. This provides many opportunities to use positional language.
	Assess the suitability of each programmable toy for outdoors depending on weather conditions and the surfaces. Outdoors offers the space to make longer, faster and noisier journeys.
Battery-operated toys	There is a wide range of battery-operated toys that are suitable for use outdoors with supervision. However, the potential of these toys needs to be carefully assessed.
Things from everyday life/the world around us	
Pelican crossings	Go for a walk and discover how to operate the pedestrian lights. In the outdoor area, set up a set of traffic lights and pelican crossing and let the children role play crossing the road safely. (Some items can be borrowed but it is fun to make your own control box by attaching jar lids and nuts and bolts to a box.)
Digital screens and electronic arrival and departure boards	Digital screens can be seen at train stations and airports. Watch a video clip or ask children about their own experiences when travelling. Role-play travelling by plane or train and checking departure time and platform/checkout number. Introduce timers and additional mark-making opportunities, such as using the chalkboard to create a personalised digital screen of where the children would like to go on holiday.
Lawnmower	Watch the grass being cut by maintenance staff or the gardener in a park and then help children construct a lawnmower from a box and broom handle with buttons and on/off switch.
Car park ticket machine	Visit a local car park or find a meter machine. Take photos or video. Talk about how the ticket machine works. Discuss what features the machine will need: clock display, coin receptacle, post it notes for tickets, etc. Introduce a car park with numbered or reserved bays and an exit barrier. Suggest that a traffic warden visits and issues tickets (add mark-making materials to the area).
ATM	Reconstruct the 'hole in the wall', using an old keyboard or numbered, laminated sheet.
	This provides many mathematical opportunities for children to remember the digits/code on their card and request money in multiples of £10.

Road digger, cement mixer	Add home-made machines to a builder's yard role-play and discuss how they work. Websites often provide useful images. Tape sounds of machines from the environment for the children to use in their play.
Visit the local laundrette/ supermarket	Look at the dials on the washing and drying machines. Talk about how long each cycle lasts and how much money is needed. Look at cash tills, bar codes, scanners, automatic doors.
For taking apart	Old keyboards, car radios, old telephones, cameras.
	NB: Pay attention to health and safety issues.

ICT resource suppliers

■ Visit www.gamesleyeec.org.uk/ict for more details of using ICT.

■ For details of Intel Digital Blue Movie Camera call TAG Learning on 01474 537887.

■ A metal detector can be purchased from Argos or from www.at-bristol.org.uk.

■ Pixie electronic toys can be purchased from Pixie, Swallow Systems, 134 Cock Lane, High Wycombe, Bucks HP13 7EA, tel: 01494 813471.

3E Resource boxes

Here are some suggestions for developing resource boxes to link with particular weather conditions or a theme following the children's interests. You can allocate a small budget to practitioners, who must then take responsibility for developing a resource box to be shared in the nursery.

Explorer's rucksack	Colour and light
Hats	Cellophane
Hand lens	Colour paddles
Maps	Translucent material
Binoculars	Coloured bottles
Torches	Twirly fabric
Disposable camera	CDs
Compass	Corkscrew hangers
Reference book	Coloured twisters
Labels & notepad	Shadow makers
Picnic	Bubbles
Rug	Coat hangers for bubble pipes
Walkie-talkies	Laminated sun catchers

Builder's box	Decorator's mates
Hard hats	Rollers
Reflective waistcoats	Squeezers
Spirit level	Brushes
Trowels	Paint trays
Fairy liquid to make cement	Water spray
Buckets	Scraper
Pulleys	Rolls of lining paper
Hooks	Buckets
Ropes	Empty tins
Mobile phone	Sandpaper
Time sheet, work schedule	Spirit level
Letter headings, forms	Tape measure

Snow and ice	Windy day
Sledge	Sari
Trays	Wind socks
Tin lids	Foil, Cellophane
Pictures of snowflakes	Poems, stories
Poems (laminated)	Photos, pictures
Books	Parachutes
Scrapers	Kites, pinwheel
Gloves	Carrier bags
Hand lens	Old umbrellas
Salt	Crepe paper
Assorted containers –different depths	Bubble blowers
Food colouring	Balloons on strings
Glitter	Chimes
	Twirling objects

Outdoor weaving	Treasure trove
Construction netting in different colours	Treasure
Strips of plastic – cut up carrier bags	Metal detector
Strips of fabric	Magnets
Strips of crepe paper	Fool's gold
Floristry ribbon	Rocks and nuggets
Tapes	Sequins
Large holed beads	Coins
Flat plastic sink drainer	Marbles
Gardening nets	Old jewellery
Climbing plant trainer	Casket
Trellis	Keys
String	Tweezers
Twine	Bags
Wool	Brushes
Pegs to hang up weavings	Clipboards
Lines to attach materials to	Labels
Vegetable netting	Trowels

Mini-beast area	Other ideas
Logs	■ Picnic hamper
Carpets	■ Stage management
Rotting leaves	■ Darkness
Books	■ Number hunt
Laminated categorisation sheets	■ Artist's box – easel, etc.
Plastic mini-beasts	■ Monsters
Sketch pads, clipboards	■ Archaeological digs
Drawing pencils	■ Laundry sack

3F Developing the potential of walls and corners

(With thanks to Michelle and Wendy, project leaders)

Weaving wall

Attach four pieces of timber to the wall. Paint them and varnish for protection. Staple gun a piece of construction netting to the wood with industrial staples. Add a storage box with scrap pieces of material, rope, string, lace, etc.

Chalk board

Measure out a section of a wall. Use PVA glue and water to prepare the surface. Paint with black paint and varnish. Add a different coloured border or wooden frame if you wish. Collect chalks and a sponge and bucket to wash the wall with water. (Magnetic paint is also available but is more expensive.)

Number bug wall

Prepare wall with PVA glue and water. Paint with gloss paint and varnish. Use Rawlplugs and hooks drilled into the wall to attach laminated numbers 1–10. Children can help design the bugs (or other features). The Number Bug wall encourages children to investigate numbers up to 10. The children count how many spots on each insect and find the correct number to hang on the hook beneath the insect. Use numbers from other community languages too.

Chime wall

Collect items such as spoons, corks, cans, plastic bottles, lids, shells and other items that make a noise when they touch each other. With adult support, children can hand drill a hole in these items and glue, stick or thread them together. Add wooden batons or metal tubing for children to experiment with the sounds that they make and listen as the wind causes them to chime.

Mini-beast area

Create a place to explore and discover real mini-beasts. Section off an area with logs. Fill it with child safe woodchip. Add a mirror with safety plastic, laminated pictures of mini-beasts and plastic mini-beasts. The children can use trowels and tweezers to investigate. They may find woodlice, earwigs, spiders and snails. Clipboards, paper, pencils, hand lenses, investigation boxes and a camera are kept in the activity box linked with this area.

3G Ideas for outdoor play during autumn, winter and early spring

(With thanks to Kathryn Solly, Chelsea Open Air Nursery)

Communication, language and literacy

- Mirror to the sky
- Cobwebs
- Raindrops and puddles
- A 'creature'
- Messages, signs and symbols
- Road safety and symbols
- Emergency role-play
- Weather recording
- Large paint brushes, giant chalk-floor, walls and paper

Mathematical development

- Number line hopscotch
- Number pathways and hunts
- Measuring bodies and equipment
- Chalk/paint numerals, shapes and sizes
- Bean bag shapes, sizes, colours and numbers
- Ordering children, bottles, leaves, natural objects
- Post office, aeroplane role play

Personal, social and emotional development

- Growing and caring for plants such as pansies, bulbs, heathers, cabbages
- Circle and parachute games
- Follow my leader, Sausages, Simon says, What's the time, Mr Wolf?
- Ball/bean bag turn taking games
- Dens
- Puppet theatre
- Role-play adventures
- Silhouettes and shadows

Knowledge and understanding of the world

- Weather chart recording
- Planting bulbs and recording growth
- Cardboard box/tube constructions
- Treasure box/bone/shell

- Chalk roadways/road safety
- Umbrellas and boots for rain/puddle science
- Drawing umbrellas, bikes, etc.
- Frost/snow science
- Floor robot
- Digital camera
- Festivals and celebrations

Physical development

- Obstacle course
- Reverse challenge, for example climb the slide
- Turn-taking games
- Air ball tennis
- Parachute
- Physio-ball
- Giant Lego bricks
- Syringes, bean bags and squeezy bottle targets
- Giant paint brushes and water

Creative development

- Chalk and large brush painting
- Huge painting on floor and wall
- Musical pathways
- Dance/drum to music
- Role-play
- Squeegee sand
- Shaving foam
- Balloon, string painting

Bibliography

Berman, L., cited in W. Titman (1994) *Special Places, Special People.* Godalming: World Wildlife Fund for Nature/Learning through Landscapes.

Bilton, H. (1998) *Outdoor Play in the Early Years: Management and Innovation.* London: David Fulton Publishers.

Bilton, H. (2004) *Playing Outside: Activities, Ideas and Inspiration for the Early Years.* London: David Fulton Publishers.

Brearley, M. (1969), cited in H. Bilton. (1998) *Outdoor Play in the Early Years: Management and Innovation.* London: David Fulton Publishers.

Browne, N. (2004) *Gender Equity in the Early Years,* Buckingham: Open University Press.

Bruce, T. (1987) *Early Childhood Education.* London: Hodder and Stoughton.

Bruce, T. (2004a) *Developing Learning in Early Education.* London: Paul Chapman Publishing.

Bruce, T. (2004b) *Cultivating Creativity in Babies, Toddlers and Young Children.* London: Hodder and Stoughton.

Bruce, T. and C. Meggitt (1996) *Child Care and Education.* London: Hodder and Stoughton.

Canadian Childcare Federation. www.cccf-fcsge.ca (accessed 20 May 2004).

Children Now (2004) *Play Charter.* www.childrennow.co.uk (accessed 25 January 2005).

Coram Family Project (2003) *Listening to Young Children.* Buckingham: Open University Press.

Cullen, J. (1993) 'Preschool children's use and perceptions of outdoor play areas', *Early Years Development and Care,* 89, 45–56.

Davies, M. (2003), cited in T. Bruce (2004a) *Developing Learning in Early Education.* London: Paul Chapman Publishing.

DfES (2003) *Growing Schools.* www.teachernet.gov.uk/growingschools (accessed 7 November 2004).

DfES/HM Government (2004) *Every Child Matters: Change for Children.* London: Department for Education and Skills. www.everychildmatters.gov.uk. (accessed 15 January 2005).

DfES/HM Treasury (2004) *Treasury Choice for Parents: the Best Start for Children: a Ten-Year Strategy for Childcare.* www.hm-treasury.gov.uk (accessed 15 January 2005).

Dickens, M. and J. Denziloe (2003) *All Together.* London: National Children's Bureau.

Dietze, B. and B. Crossley. *Opening the Door to the Outdoors.* www.cccf-fcsge.ca/practice/programming/opentooutdoors.en.htm (accessed 4 April 2004).

Dietz, W.H. (2001) 'The obesity epidemic in young children', *British Medical Journal,* 322 (7282), 313–14.

Edgington, M. (2003) *The Great Outdoors: Developing Children's Learning Through Outdoor Provision, (2nd Ed.)* London: British Association for Early Childhood Education.

Gallahue, D. and J. Ozmun (1998), cited in J. Riley (ed.) (2003) *Learning in the Early Years.* London: Paul Chapman Publishing.

Goddard-Blyth, S. (2000) 'First steps to the most important ABC', *Times Educational Supplement,* 7 January, 23.

Goswami, U. (2004) 'Neuroscience and education', *British Journal of Educational Psychology,* 74. 1–14.

Greenman, J. and A. Stonehouse (1996) *Prime Times: A Handbook for Excellence in Toddler Care.* St Paul, MN: Redleaf Press.

Henniger, M. (1985) cited in J. Riley (ed.) (2003) *Learning in the Early Years.* London: Paul Chapman Publishing.

House of Commons Select Committee (January 2001) *First Report – Early Years.* London: Education and Employment Committee Publications.

Isaacs, S. (1954) *The Educational Value of the Nursery School.* London: British Association for Early Childhood Education.

John, A. and R. Wheway (2004) *Can Play, Will Play: Playgrounds for Disabled Children.* London: National Playing Fields Association.

Kennington, L. (2005) *Young Children and Technology.* London: British Association for Early Childhood Education.

Learning through Landscapes (undated) *Groundnotes for Discovery: Outdoor Provision for Early Years.* Winchester: Learning through Landscapes.

Lewisham Early Years Advice and Resource Network (2002) *A Place to Learn.* London: PDA Design & Advertising.

McMillan, M. (1930), cited in M. Ouvry (2001) 'All about outdoor learning', *Nursery World,* 5 April 2001, 15–22.

Mears, K. (1997), cited in H. Tovey. (1999) 'A unique educational experience', *Early Years Educator,* 1(7). i–viii.

Montessori, M. (1988) *The Discovery of the Child.* Oxford: Clio Press.

Norris, S. (2004) 'The extinction of experience', *Conserver,* Spring 2004, 6–9.

Ofsted (2001) *Full Day Care: Guidance to the National Standards.* Nottingham: DfES Publications.

Ouvry, M. (2000) *Exercising Muscles and Minds: Outdoor Play and the Early Years Curriculum.* London: The National Early Years Network.

Ouvry, M. (2001) 'All about outdoor learning', *Nursery World,* 5 April, 15–22.

Play Safety Forum (2004) 'Managing risk in play provision'. www.ncb.org.uk (accessed 26 January 2005).

Pellegrini, A. (1998) BBC Horizon, Fat Files Special: Born to be Fat/Fixing Fat/Living on Air.

Qualifications and Curriculum Authority (2000) *Curriculum Guidance for the Foundation Stage.* London: QCA.

Reilly *et al.* (1999) *Cancer Prevention: A Resource to Support Local Action in Delivering the NHS Cancer Plan.* London: NHS Health Development Agency.

Siraj-Blatchford, J. (2003) *More than Computers.* London: British Association of Early Education.

Stoneham, J. (1996) *Grounds for Sharing: A Guide to Developing Special School Sites.* Winchester: Learning through Landscapes.

SureStart (2003) *Birth to Three Matters.* London: Department for Education and Skills.

Thomas, G. and G. Thompson (2004) *A Child's Place: Why Environment Matters to Children.* London: Green Alliance. Demos www.demos.co.uk (accessed 3 December 2004).

Titman, W. (1994) *Special Places, Special People.* Godalming: World Wildlife Fund for Nature/Learning through Landscapes.

Tovey, H. (1999) 'A unique educational experience', *Early Years Educator,* 1(7), i–viii.

Viner, R. and M. Hotopf (2004) 'Childhood predictors of self reported chronic fatigue syndrome/myalgic encephalomyelitis in adults'. www.bmj.bmjjournals.com (accessed 13 October 2004).

Walker, M. (2003) 'Risky business', *Out of School,* June, 8–9.

www.standards.dfes.gov.uk/primary/foundationstage (accessed 22 January 2005).

Useful contacts

Association Kokopelli

Address: Ripple Farm, Crundale, Canterbury, Kent CT4 TEB
Website: www.organicseedonline.com

Catalogue of traditional varieties of vegetable, many on the brink of extinction

British Trust for Conservation Volunteers (BTCV)

Address: 163 Balby Road, Balby, Doncaster SN4 0RH
Telephone: 01302 572244
Website: www.bctv.org.uk

Small grants available

Children's Play Council

Address: 8 Wakley Street, London EC1V 7QE
Telephone: 020 7843 6016

A national alliance of organisations interested in children's play

Free Play Network

Address: c/o Playlink, The Co-op Centre, 11 Mowill Street, London SW9 6BG
Website: www.freeplaynetwork.org.uk

Promotes better play opportunities for children

Fox Project

Address: The Old Chapel Bradford Street, Tonbridge, Kent TN9 1AW
Telephone: 01732 367397, Fox Deterrent Helpline 0906 272 441

Froglife

Address: Mansion House, 27–28 Market Place, Halesworth, Suffolk IP19 8AY
Telephone: 01986 873733
Website: www.froglife.org.uk

Landlife

Address: Court Hey Park, Liverpool L16 3NA
Telephone: 0151 737 1819
Website: www.landlife.org.uk

Wildfower conservation charity working mainly in urban areas

Learning through Landscapes

Address: 3rd Floor, Southside Offices, Law Courts, Winchester SO23 8DL
Telephone: 01962 846258
Website: www.ltl.org.uk

Works with early years settings, schools and organisations across the country to help them improve and develop their grounds

Mindstretchers

Address: The Warehouse, Rossie Place, Auchterarder, Perthshire PH3 1AJ
Telephone: 01746 664409
Website: www.mindstretchers.co.uk

Produces a range of resources for outdoor play

Royal Horticultural Society

Address: Education Department, Wisley, Woking, Surrey GU23 6QB
Telephone: 01483 224234
Website: www.rhs.org.uk/education/schoolscheme.asp

Offers a School Membership Scheme free of charge. Its benefits include:

■ a termly newsletter, written specifically for teachers and schoolchildren
■ reduced rates for INSET courses
■ advice on gardening issues
■ eligibility for the RHS School Members Seed Distribution Scheme.

Royal Society for the Protection of Birds (RSPB)

Address: The Lodge, Sandy, Bedfordshire SG13 2DL
Telephone: 01767 680551
Website: www.rspb.org.uk

Tree for All

Address: Woodland Trust, Autumn Park, Grantham, Lincolnshire NG31 6LL
Telephone: 01476 581106
Website: www.treeforall.org.uk

Gives the children the chance to understand nature and the power to care for it. The campaign aims to involve one million children in directly planting trees through schools and community groups.

Wiggly Wigglers

Address: Lower Blakemere Farm, Blakemere, Herefordshire HR2 9PX
Telephone: 01981 500391
Website: www.wigglywigglers.co.uk

For gardening, wildlife ponds, natural pest control, composting

Wildlife Trusts

Website: www.wildlifetrusts.org

Trusts based in the UK can give advice on matters concerning wildlife and planting.

Index

action plans 11–16

active play 56–8l; bicycles 58; climbing, crawling and balancing 57; reflecting 58–9; running 56

areas of learning xv

art ephemera 63–5

benefits of outdoor play 75–8; for children 75–7; in learning 76–7; for parents 78; for practitioners 77

Brent Early Years Annual Conference 2003 xvii, xviii, xx

Brent Outdoor Play Project xvii–xxii

carers see parents

checklists: downloadable 79; observation 80; self-evaluation of outdoor play 80–4

climbing, crawling and balancing 57

clothing for outdoor play 13, 18

communication 52–6; language and literacy xvii, 99; mark-making 54; talking and cooperating – sharing ideas 54–6; writing 52

community involvement 19

construction 61–2, 65–6

corners 98

creative development xviii, 100

cross-curricular learning 46–7

Curriculum Guidance, Foundation Stage xvii, xix

developing outdoor play areas 1–9; complete overhaul 1–4; imaginative play area 9; long-term plan 4–6; quick-change approach 6, 8; response to Ofsted inspection 6, 7; staff training 5, 6, 8; using recycled items 8

developing outdoor project, initial processes 86

disabilities xx, 74

Early Learning Goals xviii

the elements: rain 60; snow 59; sun 61; wind 60

exploring and investigating: bubbles 51; extending play 48; mini beasts 46–8; planting 52; water 48–50

family members see parents

finances 3, 16–17, 20, 73

floor plans 13

found materials 63, 87–9

gender, outdoor learning xx

higher-order thinking 65–6

ICT 92–5

imaginative play 65

independent learning 43

information sharing 5, 6

knowledge and understanding of the world xviii, 99–100

lack of outdoor play, consequences for learning xix–xx

learning bays 25–8; creative area 29–33; digging area 39; environmental area 37; growing area 40; imaginative play area 35–6; open space area 41–3; quiet area 34; wild area 38

learning benefits of outdoor play 76–7

learning opportunities 46–8, 51, 52, 54, 56–9, 61, 62, 63, 65–6

learning outdoors: art ephemera 63–5; communication 52–6; construction 61–2; elements, the 59–61; exploring and investigating 45–66; higher-order thinking 65–6; role play 62–3

mathematics xvii, 99

mini beasts 46–8, 98

movement: and child development xix–xx; running 56

music 33

natural materials 90–1

obesity xx–xix
Ofsted, need to develop outdoor learning xviii
outdoor learning, advantages 45, 75–8

parents: benefits of outdoor play 78; fundraising 20; involving 20–3; practical help 20; as problem 73; raising understanding 20–3
personal, social and emotional learning xvii, 99
physical development xviii, 100
The Play Charter xvii
playing out xviii
predictable environment 26
problems introducing outdoor learning 67–74; foxes 72; vandalism 67

quiet time 58–9

recycling 17, 87–9
research findings: food xviii–xix; gender xx; movement xix; playing out xviii
resource boxes 96–7
resourcing the outdoor area 16–18

restricted space 70–1
risk management 73–4
role play 62–3

seasons 99
self-evaluation of outdoor play 81–4
sharing ideas 54–6
sharing space 68–9
staff: benefits of outdoor play 77; changes in attitude 24; reluctance to change 69; role in outdoor learning 23–4; training 5, 6, 8
statutory requirements xvii–xviii
stereotypical play xx
storage 19; problems 69–70; trolleys and drawers 25–7
sun protection 18
sustained shared thinking 56

visits: garage 63; local area 71; local shops 93

walls 98
water 32, 48–51, 89
weather 59–61; as problem 72

9 781843 123507